IFLA

International Federation of Library Associations and Institutions
Fédération Internationale des Associations de Bibliothécaires et des Bibliothèques
Internationaler Verband der bibliothekarischen Vereine und Institutionen
Международная Федерация Библиотечных Ассоциаций и Учреждений

IFLA Publications 21

Françoise Hébert
and
Wanda Noel

Copyright and Library Materials for the Handicapped

A Study prepared for the International Federation of Library Associations and Institutions.

K·G·Saur München·New York·London·Paris 1982

IFLA Publications
edited by Willem R. H. Koops

Recommended catalog entry:

Hébert, Françoise
Copyright and library materials for the handicapped /
a study prepared for the International Federation
of Library Associations and Institutions; by
Françoise Hébert and Wanda Noel. – New York etc.:
K. G. Saur, 1982. – 111 p.; 21 cm. – (IFLA Publications;
21)
ISBN 3-598-20381-0

K. G. SAUR Verlag KG
Pössenbacherstrasse 2 b
Postfach 71 10 09
D-8000 München 71
Federal Republic of Germany
Tel. (089) 79 89 01
Telex 521 2067 saur d

K. G. SAUR S.A.R.L.
38, Rue de Bassano
F-75008 Paris
Tél. 723.55.18
Telex 630144 iso bur

K. G. SAUR Ltd.
Shropshire House
2–20 Capper Street
London WC1E 6JA
Tel. (01) 637 15 71

Distributed in the
United States and Canada by:
Shoe String Press Inc.
P.O.Box 4327
995 Sherman Avenue
Hamden, Connecticut 06514
Tel. 001-203-248-6307

CIP-Kurztitelaufnahme der Deutschen Bibliothek

Hébert, Françoise:
Copyright and library materials for the
handicapped : a study prepared for the Internat. Fed.
of Library Assoc. and Inst. / Françoise
Hébert and Wanda Noel. – München ; New York ;
London ; Paris : Saur, 1982.
(IFLA publications ; 21)
ISBN 3-598-20381-0

NE: Noel, Wanda:; International Federation
of Library Associations and Institutions:
IFLA publications

ISSN 0344-6891 (IFLA publications)

Published by K. G. Saur Verlag KG, München

Printed in the Federal Republic of Germany
by Hain-Druck GmbH, Meisenheim/Glan

ISBN 3-598-20381-0

TABLE OF CONTENTS

PREAMBLE

This study was prepared for the International Federation of Library Associations and Institutions, through a grant from the Council on Library Resources in Washington, D.C., U.S.A.

It examines the special nature of library services for the handicapped, and identifies copyright problems associated with the production and dissemination of materials in braille, audiotape and large print. Copyright laws which have special provisions for the handicapped and international copyright conventions are examined to determine the types of legislative action which are possible and practical to resolve copyright problems. A series of recommendations for IFLA action, and for action at other levels, concludes the study.

The chapters dealing with copyright legislation were researched and written by Wanda M. Noel, B.A., L.L.B., Barrister and Solicitor. Ms. Noel is the 1980 winner of the prestigious International Law Prize, sponsored by the Confédération Internationale des Sociétés des Auteurs et Compositeurs (CISAC), for a research paper on Compulsory Licences and Copyright, an area of direct import for copyright and materials for the handicapped.

A number of colleagues acted as advisors to this Study, providing useful comments, critiques and suggestions to the first draft. Their contribution was positive, and is gratefully acknowledged.

Anders Arnor, Honorary Secretary General, W.C.W.B. Sweden.
F.K. Cylke, Director, National Library Services for the Blind and Physically Handicapped, U.S. Library of Congress.
Peter Ditz, Chairman, Tape Aids for the Blind. South Africa.
Dorina de Gouvea Nowill, President, W.C.W.B. Brazil.
A.A.Keyes, Copyright Advisor, Department of the Secretary of State, Canada.
John Larsen, State Library and Printing House for the Blind. Denmark
Graham Laurence, Royal Blind Society of New South Wales, Australia.
Anna Ubostad, Chairman, IFLA Round Table on Libraries for the Blind and Librarian, Norwegian Association of the Blind.
From IFLA Headquarters, Margreet Wijnstroom and
A.L. van Wesemael provided direction and support.

Special thanks to A.A.Keyes, who stimulated my interest in copyright and to Bev. Cooke, who keeps me organized. My appreciation to th Canadian National Institute for the Blind for their supportive and understanding attitude during the time I spent on this study.

Françoise Hébert

1. THE HANDICAPPED POPULATION

Print surrounds us, and most of us take it for granted. We scan the daily newspapers, we subscribe to current magazines, we purchase books from bookstores and borrow them from public libraries. At school, at work or at play, we consult manuals, textbooks, reports and schedules. Our society depends largely on print for the transfer of information and the communication of knowledge. Access to print is vital in a print-oriented society.

Persons unable to read print because of a physical handicap constitute a small but significant portion of the world population. Physical handicaps which prevent the reading of print can be grouped into three broad categories:

1. Visual Impairment

   Persons who are totally without sight, or whose visual impairment, with correction and regardless of optical measurement, prevents the reading of standard printed material.

2. Motor Impairment

   Persons physically impaired to the extent that they are incapable of reading normal print or holding a book or turning its pages. This includes persons who have paralysis, muscular dystrophy, cerebral palsy or other motor disabilities of a temporary or permanent nature.

3. Neurological Impairment

   Persons who have a neurological dysfunction of an organic nature, resulting in an inability to interpret or understand printed words or sentences.

While the exact number of persons unable to read print because of a physical handicap is unknown, statistics exist for certain countries and can serve as a base to estimate the worldwide incidence of reading disabilities.

In the United States of America, a recent study prepared for the Library of Congress National Library Service for the Blind and Physically Handicapped by the American Foundation for the Blind,[1] determined that approximately 1.2% of the American population is unable to read or use regular print because of a physical handicap. Applying American statistics to the world population will not result in an accurate estimate of the number of persons physically unable to use regular print, but might establish a possible minimum figure. If the world population currently stands at 4,387,000,000,[2] then a minimum estimate of the number of persons unable to read print because of a physical handicap is 57,031,000. Taking into account lower levels of medical care in less developed countries, a more realistic estimate might be closer to 75 million persons.

The AFB study discovered that in the United States, the great majority of persons with print limitations (83%) are visually impaired. A significant number (54%) have multiple reading limitations, or limitations of several types. Persons unable to read print because of a visual handicap tend to be older. In Canada, a study of legally blind persons registered with the Canadian National Institute for the Blind reveals the following age classification:[3]

AGE CLASSIFICATION OF PERSONS REGISTERED WITH CNIB CANADA 1979

0 - 5	1.5%
6 - 15	4.8%
10 - 19	2.6%
20 - 29	8 %
30 - 39	7.4%
40 - 49	7.3%
50 - 64	16.8%
65 - 80	26.6%
81	25 %

More than half the legally blind population in Canada is over 65 years of age. A significant number among the elderly are also hearing impaired. The number of elderly persons unable to read print because of visual impairment is likely to increase. At the same time, the number of younger handicapped persons is expected to decrease in the future, partly because of society's changing demographic configuration, with its declining birthrates and longer life expectancy, and because more sophisticated prevention and health care programs will also contribute to a decline in the incidence of visual impairment among young people. Degenerative diseases associated with aging may, in future, be the major causes of visual impairments which reduce an individual's ability to read printed materials.

2. SOCIAL CONSEQUENCES

Handicapped people today want, and are expected to take, an active, positive role in the society in which they live, to be educated, to hold a job, to use their abilities to the fullest extent. This was not always so. In the pre-Christian era, "blindness was looked upon as the worst evil that could befall man, and often as a punishment. Though certain blind persons attained a sort of spiritual pre-eminence..., the great mass was looked upon as practically useless, and some were at times given over for destruction. While feelings of humanity offered some a tolerable existence, the majority led the wretched life of beggars".[4]

The systematic education of visually handicapped persons began in 1784, when Valentin Haüy founded the first school for the blind in Paris. Concluding that something must be done to make the arts and sciences more accessible to the blind, Haüy invented embossed printing. Soon after, Louis Braille developed a simple, convenient and flexible writing system based on embossed dots that permitted a blind person to write with ease and read what had been written.

From then on, the inability to read printed materials because of a physical handicap stopped being synonymous with illiteracy and the world of books was open to persons who could not read print.

The formal education of persons unable to read print because of a physical handicap is now common in developed and many newly industrialised countries. Handicapped children attend special or regular schools. They are successfully completing graduate courses in law, medicine, social work, library science and many other fields.

More and more, handicapped persons are seeking and obtaining positions which require access to information normally available only in print. Doctors, lawyers, musicians, writers, systems analysts, business people, and librarians who are handicapped need access to printed information without which their job cannot be effectively done.

In addition to their requirements for educational and vocational information, handicapped persons have another important need for printed material. The United Nations Declaration of Human Rights states in Article 27 that:

> "Everyone has the right freely to participate in the cultural life of the community, to enjoy the arts and share in scientific advancement and its benefits."

In today's world, much of the richness of our cultural life is expressed in books and periodicals. Reading informs, stimulates and challenges. It provides a depth to life, a dimension so wide that it can encompass Shakespeare, Tolstoy, Molière, Agatha Christie, Arthur Hailey and Colette. Reading for pleasure adds quality to life. Persons unable to read because of a physical handicap must not be denied the benefits and pleasures that reading can bring.

If society can provide handicapped individuals with information in a form which they can use, then the debilitative effects of their handicap will be minimized, a major barrier to their successful education and employment will have been removed, and a fuller, more independent life will become possible.

SPECIAL READING MEDIA

Persons unable to read print because of a physical handicap need information transcribed into another medium which they can use. The alternate media commonly used today are braille, large print and audiotape.

Braille

Braille is a writing system based on a series of raised dots embossed on paper. Composed of 63 possible combinations of one to six dots arranged in a six position cell, braille characters can represent letters, words, numbers, punctuation, composition signs and graphic symbols. Braille is used in 71 languages ranging from Afrikaanse to Zulu. There are special braille codes for music and mathematics, and different grades of braille, each one increasing in complexity.

Blind children often become "fluent" in braille, especially if they attend schools for the blind where braille is the normal learning medium. Persons who become blind as adults and who switch over from reading by sight to reading by touch, are often slow braille readers who may prefer audiotape for leisure reading. People who lose their sight when they are elderly have difficulty in mastering braille, and the great majority do not attempt it.

The number of persons who read braille in the world today is surprisingly small, and may actually be declining as audiotape becomes more widely available. In Canada and the U.S.A., only about 1% of the handicapped population reads braille. Although often preferred to other media by those who are fluent in it, braille is likely to remain a small, specialized medium of communication.

Braille can be produced by hand, printing presses and computer. Although technological advances are making braille faster and, less expensive to produce, the small size of the present and potential braille-reading public cannot sustain a commercial market for braille materials. The production of braille, by its very nature, will probably remain a subsidized, albeit essential endeavour, directed mainly to the provision of educational and vocational support materials.

3.2 Audiotape

Audiotape is a relatively recent medium of communication for persons unable to read print because of a physical handicap. Although verbal/aural communication has always played a vital role in the life of handicapped persons, it was not until the 1930's that recorded material became widely available.

The major advantage of audiotape over braille is that no special training is required to understand it. Thus it can be used by anyone unable to read print except for those who also have hearing impairments. The major disadvantage of tape is its sequential, passive nature, which imposes the presence of a third person, the narrator, between a reader and a text. Another disadvantage which needs to be considered in the educational context, is that audiotape does not teach spelling, and may produce a generation of handicapped students who can express themselves orally but who cannot spell.

Despite these disadvantages, recorded or "talking books", as they have come to be known, have opened up the world of books to millions of individuals who could not and would never read braille.

Talking books can be produced in various formats such as reel tapes, 8 track cassettes, compact or commercial cassettes and audiodiscs. Each of these can, in turn, be produced in "closed" or "open" systems. Closed systems require special playback equipment not generally available for purchase from retail sources. Cassettes or discs recorded at unusual speeds, or specially designed cassettes, are considered "closed" systems because they require players which the public does not normally have access to. Agencies which produce talking books in closed systems have usually selected this route because they wish to guarantee controlled access to their talking books, or because the special equipment provides definite cost/benefit advantages in production and handling. The U.S. Library of Congress National Library Service for the Blind and Physically Handicapped, the Canadian National Institute for the Blind, and the Royal National Institute for the Blind in Great Britain, among others, are agencies which produce talking books in closed formats. In each case, handicapped readers must be provided with, or must purchase from exclusive sources, the appropriate special playback equipment.

Talking books in open systems are produced on records, reels or cassettes which can be played on standard, commonly available equipment. Generally, producers of talking books on open systems do not wish to limit the use of their materials, or they will limit their use through controls other than exclusive equipment. Open systems do not require that readers be provided with, or be required to purchase, special playback equipment. Most European agencies serving the handicapped, as well as all commercial publishers of talking books, have elected to produce talking books on open systems.

The existence of various types of recording formats and systems has resulted in the complication of format incompatibility, which limits the distribution of talking books, and requires that handicapped readers who wish to use tape materials from various sources, amass a veritable arsenal of playback equipment.

There is a small commercial market of talking books on cassettes and records, limited generally to best-selling books or literary or dramatic classics, or the edited versions of these. The number of titles available commercially, although growing rapidly, is insufficient to provide a broad based collection of reading materials for handicapped persons, and must be supplemented by recordings from other sources, usually government or private agencies, which produce recordings specifically for handicapped persons.

3.3 Large Print

Large type materials are usually set in 14 to 18 point type size, and feature heavy leading, simple type style and clean layout. Large print may be typeset, a method used by many commercial producers; typewritten, a method used by volunteers to meet individual needs for specific texts, or photographically enlarged.

The number of handicapped persons who can read large print materials is significantly large. There is some controversy, however, over whether large print materials are desirable, or whether magnifiers should be used to aid in reading normally printed materials, especially to serve educational and vocational needs.

There is a developing and quite substantial trade market for large print books. Several thousand English titles, and thousands more in other languages, are available from publishers, bookstores and libraries. They are used mainly by elderly persons whose vision is failing.

4. PRODUCTION OF MATERIALS FOR THE HANDICAPPED

Libraries usually build their collections by acquiring materials published by publishers. Libraries for the handicapped find themselves in an entirely different situation. Because there is, as yet, no publishing industry systematically producing large quantities of materials in audio or braille formats, libraries wishing to acquire materials in special media to serve their handicapped readers have often had to produce those materials themselves. The production of materials for the handicapped is geared to serve two distinct reader needs.

4.1 Transcription Services

The first need requires a transcription service, where materials in alternate media are produced in response to specific requests from a reader. Textbooks, research materials, reports and any other documents required to support educational, vocational and professional endeavours are produced for handicapped readers in whatever form they require. Normally, a master transcription is made from print into braille, audiotape or large type. A copy is made for loan to or retention by the handicapped reader, and the master transcription is stored in the event of further requests for that particular text. Transcription services are required to braille, record or produce in large print a wide variety of materials, which can range from elementary school texts to advanced treatises on scientific subjects. The number of copies required of any one transcription may be as few as one, or as many as several hundred, spread out over several years. The probability of a publishing industry developing to serve this particular highly specialised, low volume need is extremely remote. Transcription services will likely remain a government or privately sponsored activity, where production and the more traditional library functions of cataloguing and circulation will remain closely linked. Recording for the Blind in New York City is a well known example of a transcription service.

4.2 Recreation/Information Services

The second need of handicapped persons is for recreation/information reading materials similar in nature to those found in public libraries, where books and periodicals in alternate media are loaned from a collection already in place. In such cases, multiple copies of a title may be required to serve large numbers of handicapped readers. The Canadian National Institute for the Blind, for example, needs between 9 and 36 copies of each title to serve its 10,000 readers. The U.S. Library of Congress will normally produce more than 1,000 copies of each title in recorded form to serve the handicapped population in that country.

Libraries which lend talking books to handicapped readers are not always producers of talking books as well. In North America for example, many public libraries have begun to acquire talking books from commercial and non-profit distributers, and are offering a standard lending service to their handicapped constituents. This is a relatively new trend however. Many libraries which lend special format books to handicapped readers are still active in original or duplicate production.

Libraries which produce materials in special formats don't often view themselves as "publishers". Indeed, most will deny any statement that they are, despite the fact that their studio-produced recordings may be made available to hundreds of libraries in dozens of different countries. They view themselves rather as intermediaries between a piece of printed information and a person who cannot use it because of a physical handicap.

Few producers of materials for the handicapped have developed formal links with the publishing industry. Similarly, libraries offering services exclusively to handicapped readers have developed the traditional library functions of organizing and disseminating their materials in isolation from the professional library community.

Prior to the 1960's, few libraries for the handicapped employed professional librarians, and few organized their collections according to accepted standards of cataloguing and classification. Networking was virtually unknown, with the notable exception of the U.S. Library of Congress, which established its service network in 1931.

Even today, a large number of libraries for the handicapped create special materials to serve only the needs of their own reading public, and will not consider their original recordings or their original braille transcriptions as a product which should be made available to serve the needs of handicapped readers elsewhere. An explanation for this compartmentalized approach can be attempted by delving into the roots of library service for the handicapped. "Most libraries for the blind started as charities", write Schauder and Cram. "Often the encouragement of charitable support is so deeply rooted in the library's origins, and so much a part of its way of life, that this factor more than any other moulds the library's conception of itself, hindering it from reconsidering its aims, its methods and its relationship to sister services." The results, according to Schauder and Cram, are the "inability of unco-ordinated charities to meet new needs; an obvious misallocation of resources through overlap with other bodies; and the widening gap between funds required (e.g. to incorporate technological advances and professionally trained staff) and the amount of money that can be raised by appeals."[5]

The situation is changing rapidly, however, as governments assume more and more responsibility for library services for the handicapped. In areas where charities or private agencies continue to produce and disseminate materials for the handicapped, there is a growing awareness of the need to provide professional products and services, to standardize, co-ordinate, rationalize and participate in network arrangements. There is a growing tendency to separate the production and circulation functions of library service to the handicapped and to recognize the value of professional affiliations with the publishing and library communities.

Library services for the handicapped are emerging from the well-intentioned but sheltered and fragmented world of religious charities, and moving toward large-scale production of special media materials, adequate bibliographic control, international loans and exchanges, and integration of special services to the handicapped as a normal responsibility of school and public libraries. This "professionalisation" of services will certainly result in better services to handicapped readers. But it will also highlight, and perhaps even exacerbate, certain problem areas such as copyright.

5. COPYRIGHT AND MATERIALS FOR THE HANDICAPPED

Librarians have generally not had to concern themselves with copyright matters, except in the area of photocopying. But librarians attempting to provide services to the handicapped are more directly involved with copyright, because of the production/publishing activities which they have had to resort to in order to serve their readers. Copyright can be a problem at two phases in library service to handicapped readers. The first is at the time of the original transcription of printed books or other materials into special formats for the handicapped, when permissions to transcribe and produce are required. The second is at the dissemination stage, usually at the international level, when further permissions may need to be obtained.

5.1 Permission for Original Transcription

In most countries of the world today, libraries and other producers of materials for the handicapped must obtain the permission of the copyright owner before a work can be transcribed into braille, large type or audiotape. Separate, specific permissions are required for the original transcription, and the making of copies of each title into another medium for the handicapped.

In the past, it often happened that producers of materials for the handicapped were unaware of copyright laws and the permission requirements. Transcriptions were simply made as they were needed. Production facilities were small, the number of copies produced of any title was limited, and distribution of the copies was restricted geographically. The activities of producing agencies were largely unknown beyond the handicapped "community".

In the last two decades, as production agencies increased in size and sophistication, the legal requirement to secure permissions became better known, and letters requesting permissions to produce books in braille or audiotape or large print were duly sent off to publishers and authors. The majority of publishers generously granted permissions without charge, and most continue to do so today. But a small number of publishers will refuse permission, or require payment in return for permissions, or attach other conditions such as format restrictions, or limitations on the number of copies produced or on their distribution.

A copyright problem is therefore the fact that permissions are not always granted, and that they may include conditions which limit services that can be offered to handicapped readers.

A further problem in securing permissions is the time and cost involved in obtaining them. Typing letters of request, tracking down difficult-to-locate copyright owners, maintaining files of permissions secured or refused, and dealing with a welter of varying conditions, is a time-consuming, expensive operation. No less expensive is the time of the publisher who must search contracts and complete permission agreements.

Delays in obtaining permissions can average 3 to 6 months in countries where specific permissions are required. When libraries are waiting for permissions to record or braille a textbook for a student, such delays are tragic and unacceptable.

Requests for permissions are normally made to publishers. But in a significant number of cases, the publisher does not hold that specific subsidiary right and so cannot authorise it. Several letters may be required before the appropriate agent is found. In the case of anthologies, where each story or poem is a separate copyright entity, anywhere from 10 to 300 letters may need to be sent; and if even one or two permission requests are refused or not replied to, the anthology cannot be transcribed.

It can be seen that securing permissions for the original transcription of a work into a special format for a handicapped person can be problematical. At the very least, it is expensive in administrative time and cost. At worst, it can result in a handicapped student not being able to obtain an essential textbook, or in an employed person being refused access to important information which is easily available in print to anyone else.

As noted earlier, most permissions are granted by copyright owners. But the fact that a copyright owner can arbitrarily withold permission for a published work to be transcribed into another medium for a handicapped reader is a situation which is unfortunate, and which should be remedied.

5.2 Permission to Redisseminate

The second problem phase for copyright and materials for the handicapped involves the dissemination of additional copies of a title to readers other than those for whom the original permission to transcribe was granted. Limitations can occur when production agencies ask for permission to transcribe a work into another format to serve a limited group of users, for example handicapped readers who are clients of that agency, or nationals of that country only.

The situation can also be caused when copyright owners grant only limited permission for the dissemination of their work to handicapped readers. Special format works for the handicapped are usually treated by publishers in the same way as printed books, for which distribution rights are divided geographically. Because copyright owners are reluctant to grant world permissions, copyright becomes a practical barrier to the distribution and exchange of materials for the handicapped. For example, if an agency in Canada produces a recording of a work by a Canadian author, and a library serving handicapped readers in New Zealand wishes to obtain a copy of this recording for its collection, the New Zealand agency must obtain the permission of the copyright owner before it can acquire even one copy of the Canadian recording. The same condition must be met by any other country wishing to import a copy of the Canadian recording.

Although supplementary permissions for wider dissemination are usually granted, the time and expense required to secure them is considerable. When only a small fraction of the world's publications can be made available in special formats for the handicapped, such administrative barriers to their production and dissemination need to be reduced or eliminated.

6. COPYRIGHT LEGISLATION

Copyright barriers can be removed in two ways: by informal agreements between copyright owners and producers of materials for the handicapped, designed to ease the flow of materials in special formats, or by legislation designed to achieve the same objective.

Informal or gentlemen's agreements are useful, and quite effective in some countries. But they are not a long term solution to a problem which exists because of copyright legislation. Where copyright barriers to the production and dissemination of library materials to the handicapped are created by legislation, then the preferred course of action for removing the barriers is to amend the appropriate copyright legislation.

Any move toward legislative action can come only after an examination of the legislation currently in place. Those countries which have enacted special provisions in their copyright laws will be identified to discover current trends. Special provisions for the benefit of other than the handicapped and the legal mechanisms used to enact special provisions will also be identified and examined. Only following such an examination can concrete recommendations be made on how best to remove copyright barriers to the production and dissemination of materials for the handicapped.

6.1 Existing Copyright Legislation

In 1979, of the 73 countries[6] party to the Berne[7] or Universal Copyright Convention[8] only 8 had enacted special provisions for the handicapped: Japan[9], Denmark[10], Finland[11], Iceland[12], Norway[13], the Soviet Union[14], Sweden[15], and the U.S.A.[16]. In the following year, 1980, Australia also enacted special provisions for the handicapped. The text of each of the provisions is reproduced in Appendix "A". In these cases, legislators have attempted to balance the needs of copyright owners with the needs of the handicapped. Provisions among the 9 countries deal variously with braille, recording, performance or display via transmissions and photography. Each of the provisions represents, in legal terms, what would otherwise be an exclusive right of the copyright owner. Thus each constitutes a derogation from the exclusive rights of the copyright owner. The rights affected by these special provisions are reproduction, publication and performance.

6.11 Reproduction

The right of reproduction is the very essence of copyright law. In fact, the English word "copyright" has its origins in the phrase "the right to copy" which is synonymous with the right to reproduce. A work protected by copyright is considered "reproduced" when it has been fixed in some material form. In this way, producers of material for the handicapped "reproduce" a copyright work each time they produce a work in braille or recorded form. Without special provisions in the relevant copyright law, or without the permission of the copyright owner, the production activity would infringe copyright, leaving the producer liable to legal action.

Except for the U.S.A., all countries which have enacted special provisions for the handicapped, included a provision for braille reproduction. Three countries (Denmark, Ireland and Norway) provided exceptions for photographic reproduction for educational use of the "deaf and sufferers from speech impediments". The new Australian legislation also deals with photographic reproduction but requires payment of equitable remuneration and ultimate use by the handicapped for research, study and instruction only.

Japan, Denmark, Finland, Norway, Sweden and Australia have enacted special provisions for the reproduction of copyright materials by means of recording for the use of the handicapped.

6.12 Publication

As with reproduction, the right to publish is normally reserved exclusively to the copyright owner. The origin of this right lies in the common sense notion that an author possesses a form of property in his creation so long as he keeps it to himself. In Iceland[17], the copyright law provides that "copies in braille may be printed and published of published literary and musical works". Similarly, the copyright law of the Soviet Union[18] provides that "the publication in braille for the blind of published works" is permissible without the consent of the author. In terms of freedom granted by special provisions, Iceland and the Soviet Union go much further that the countries which permit reprography by means such as braille, recording or photography, because the right to publish means the right to issue copies to the public[19]. While the right to publish applies only to braille copies, an extension of this right to recordings would supply a user category beyond the visually handicapped. An example would be the production of recordings of top selling literary works on cassettes for use while driving.

6.13 Performance

Special provisions dealing with the rights of performance and display are unique to the copyright law of the United States of America[20]. Limitations on the exclusive rights of the copyright owner take the form of exceptions from liability for certain performances and displays of certain programming intended for the disabled and the visually handicapped. As most of the provisions relate to activities not normally carried on by libraries, for example the communication by performance of audio visual material, they are of little assistance to producers of material primarily intended as a substitute for print. There is, however, an application here for the broadcast of material on a radio reading service for the handicapped.

6.14 Who May Act Under the Special Provisions

Who may act under the special provisions varies widely in the nine countries identified. In some cases, the benefit of the provisions is limited to libraries and establishments for the promotion of the welfare of the blind. In other jurisdictions, for example in Sweden, anyone, including for example a commercial recording studio or an individual, can utilize the special provision provided that a handicapped person is the ultimate beneficiary.

6.15 Works Subject to the Special Provision

The only characteristic common to the nine countries identified[21] is that the special provisions apply only to published, as opposed to unpublished works. In some cases, the application is further restricted to published literary, dramatic and musical works, as opposed to any and all works.

6.16 Conditions to the Special Provisions

What has been referred to as "special provisions" are in fact special because of the category of user to which the provision relates. All provisions refer to the existence of a handicap. The terminology used varies and includes: blind, disabled, seriously disabled persons, persons who cannot attend school or similar places because of a disability or special circumstance, handicapped persons who are unable to read normal printed material as a result of this handicap, the deaf, handicapped persons who are unable to hear the aural signals accompanying the transmission of visual signals, sufferers from speech impediments, sufferers from defective vision and those unable to read ordinary books due to their disability.

Concerning the use of the materials produced, various conditions allow them to be used exclusively for the purpose of lending for the use of the blind; use without commercial advantage; and use for educational purposes. These conditions are, in the usual course, designed to balance the legitimate interests of both the handicapped user and the copyright owner. The same is also true with respect to the question of remuneration.

6.17 Remuneration

In seven of the eight jurisdictions which contain a

special provision with respect to reproduction in braille, no payment is required. The only exception is found in Australia where braille reproduction is subject to the payment of equitable remuneration at the request of the copyright owner. The same is not the case with respect to reproduction by recording means. In Denmark and Norway "remuneration" and "compensation" are respectively required. In Australia the owner of the copyright has the right to request "equitable remuneration". In Norway, the compensation is defrayed by the state. In Denmark the provision is silent concerning who is responsible for the remuneration which therefore requires the person or organization who acts under the special provision to assume that responsibility. In Australia "the body administering an institution assisting handicapped readers", who carries out the reproduction, is responsible for payment. In all cases it is the "author" of the work recorded who is entitled to the "remuneration". In Japan, Finland and Sweden, no payment is required for reproduction by means of recording.

No rationale is apparent as to whether or not remuneration should be required for reproduction by means of recording. Out of six countries which have enacted this kind of special provision, three require compensation to be paid and three do not.

Arguments for both sides can be persuasively made, as is evidenced by the fact that no consistent pattern has emerged. This matter appears to be primarily subjective in nature, depending on whether the legislative body construes the social objective to be served by the special provision as justifying reproduction and public performance without remuneration.

6.2 Special Provisions for Analogous Purposes

In those countries where copyright becomes a barrier to the provision of materials to handicapped readers, attempting to change the law in order to eliminate the barriers seems an obvious and desirable objective. Other interest groups have not hesitated to put forward their arguments for special provisions, and a sampling of special provisions with respect to other uses illustrates that the handicapped have not been alone in obtaining special provisions on their behalf.

The characteristic common to all special use provisions is that each represents, on one hand, a derogation from the rights of the creator of the work and, on the other hand, a benefit for a special genus of user. Provisions of this kind are presumably enacted to meet a defined socially desirable objective which the domestic legislative body has deemed, for reasons presented to it, to merit enactment into law. There appears to be no restrictions on the rights or the type of copyright work which can be affected by such provisions, nor the extent to which the derogation can go.

The variety of special provisions illustrates that beneficiaries other than the handicapped, have obtained special status under copyright law. A representative selection of special provisions includes:

- Library Use. In the Italian Copyright Law[22], photocopying of works in libraries, when made for personal use or for the services of the library, is free of any copyright restrictions. In Tunisia[23], the department in charge of cultural affairs may, in cases of need, authorize public libraries to reproduce literary, scientific or artistic works in the necessary number and limited to the needs of their activities, subject to equitable remuneration, to be fixed in the absence of agreement by a commission appointed by the government.

- Use by Agricultural Fairs. In Canada[24], it is not an infringement of the exclusive rights of the copyright owner to perform a musical work, without motive of gain, at an agricultural fair.
- Educational Use:

  (i) In Pakistan[25] copyright does not subsist in a variety of works, including literary works, as regards their reprint, translation, adaptation or publication by or under the authority of the Federal government for purposes of teaching, study or research in educational institutions as textbooks.

  (ii) Free use of music for educational purposes is found in the Austrian copyright law[26]. The free use includes multiplication and distribution of single published songs in compilations destined for teaching in schools.

  (iii) And finally in Cuba[27] neither authorization nor payment of remuneration is required to utilize, subject to certain conditions, even entire works if justified by their briefness or character for the purpose of teaching.
- Religious Use. In Finland[28] a published work may be publicly performed at divine services without the authorization of, or remuneration to, the owner of the performance rights.
- Personal Use:

  (i) In Yugoslavia[29] the reproduction of published works for the purposes of improving one's personal knowledge is free provided that such reproduction is neither intended for nor accessible to the public.

- (ii) Similarly in Egypt[30], if a person, for his strictly personal use, reproduces a single copy of a work which has already been published, the author cannot oppose his action.

A continued listing of sampled special provisions would belabour the point. Instead, a listing of common socially desirable objectives served by special provisions randomly selected throughout the jurisdictions examined will suffice. The objectives include, but are not limited to, the following: charitable, economic, political, social, judicial, news reporting, and legislative purposes and range from publication and reproduction through to communication by broadcasting methods. The purpose of the presentation of the special provisions and the listing of the social objectives commonly the subject of special provisions illustrates the wide variety of activities, concerning works protected by copyright, which are carried out under special legal provisions covering those activities.

The activities deemed socially desirable and for which special provisions exist include such things as the free performance of music at agricultural fairs as well as less esoteric objectives such as charitable and religious objects. Special provisions dealing with the production of material for the benefit of the handicapped can be included, it is submitted with logical consistency, within any sampling or listing of socially desirable objectives. The performance of music at agricultural fairs is certainly no less socially desirable or necessary than the production of material for the handicapped.

The production of material for the handicapped, in many instances, takes place for educational purposes. Therefore, in those jurisdictions with special provisions dealing with reproduction or public performance for educational purposes, the producers of material for the handicapped may not require further special provisions for at least the educational portion of their activities. In this case they may act with impunity under the wider provision dealing with educational use. Some form of special status may also be available under general exceptions such as fair use or fair dealing depending on the scope of the activities permitted under such provisions in each jurisdiction.

The definition of what is socially desirable and therefore meriting a special provision in a copyright law is a matter which must, in the final analysis, be determined by the jurisdictions concerned. That determination is not of a legal nature but rather is subjective in character. However, the ability of any jurisdiction to act upon a determination to enact special provisions for some socially desirable purpose, including for the handicapped and for the producers of material for them, is constrained by the international obligations of the jurisdiction concerned. The Berne and Universal Copyright Conventions regulate, to a large extent, the legal mechanisms which can and cannot be used in the domestic legislation of member countries. The legal mechanisms which are utilized in the special provisions of the legislation of the countries examined are varied. These mechanisms, with examples and illustrations where necessary, are examined next.

6.3 Legal Mechanisms

As the various special provisions being discussed are limitations placed upon exclusive copyright rights it is necessary to define copyright in order to define that which limits it. In general terms copyright is a number of exclusive rights granted to the creators of literary, scientific and artistic works for a limited period of time. A special provision in these terms can be defined as a statutory consent to do what would otherwise be illegal. In sociological terms a special provision can be defined as an attempt to balance the interest of the creator in exploiting and controlling his creation and the public interest in having access to the products of the intellect.

In a broad sense the term "copyright" is inadequate in today's world[31]. Its origins lie rooted in print technology where use by copying was the major means of reproduction. In other systems the rights have been associated with the persona of the author, apart from the work. Today, author's rights in their creations include performance, exhibition, adaptation and broadcasting of works on the basis that these acts are alternative and sometimes the more important means of exploitation. Ladas, for example, points out that the German "Urhebessecht" and the French "droit d'auteur" are more generically descriptive of the expanding concept, the English equivalent of which should be "author's rights"[32].

Copyright means, in universal terms, legal rights to prohibit unauthorized use. The rights are limited in time and are assignable.[33] While such a general definition of copyright is not controversial, agreement usually stops at that point. Each jurisdiction has made its own determination as to the particular meaning of the extent and scope of copyright rights and to what material and persons the rights attach[34].

In considering action at the legislative level to ease or eliminate problems which exist in respect of copyright and materials for the handicapped, several legal mechanisms need to be examined and defined. These mechanisms have been used to enact special provisions for the handicapped, and for other special provisions as well, in legislation currently in place in various countries.

6.31 Exception

An exception to copyright protection permits the use of copyright material without either the authorization of, or payment to, the owner of the copyright. Seven of the eight jurisdictions which provide special provisions with respect to braille reproduction do so by providing an exception, that is, neither authorization or payment is required. Sweden, Japan and Finland provide exceptions for reproduction by recording for the benefit of the handicapped.

6.32 Compulsory Licence

A compulsory licence[35] permits use without the authorization of the owner of the copyright for specified purposes but requires payment for that use. Copyright means, in general terms, exclusive rights to prohibit unauthorized use. Compulsory licensing as a limitation on exclusive rights results in the use of copyright material which otherwise would be a matter of negotiation and either refusal or authorization. This limitation reduces exclusive rights to rights of remuneration and invests a user with a so-called "right to use". A compulsory licence permits the use of a creator's work without authorization provided certain conditions are met and royalties paid. The types of conditions vary with jurisdictions but, in general, the compulsory licence restricts (1) the persons with whom copyright owner must contract; (2) the times of contracting; and (3) the royalty which is set by an independent body, according to particular criteria. The most pervasive example of such a licence is that going to the mechanical reproduction of music by sound recordings. By definition the licence cannot be exclusive, nor can the time of the licence be effectively limited except by the general term of copyright, upon the expiration of which no licence is then needed. The royalty is that fixed by statute or from time to time by an appropriate authority. Norway and Denmark have enacted compulsory licensing provisions for the reproduction by recording for visually handicapped and disabled users.

6.33 Arbitration

This refers to a special provision which appoints a neutral regulatory organization to set remuneration for the use of a work where the owner and user cannot agree. In this case exclusive rights exist until there is failure to reach an agreement following which an arbitration procedure becomes operative.

Two examples, one from the United States of America as a Universal Copyright Convention country and one from Japan as both a Berne and Universal Copyright Convention country, will illustrate this arbitration mechanism. In the United States of America's copyright law section 118 provides for use of certain works by non-commercial educational broadcasting stations. The fees and other terms and conditions for this use are not set out in the copyright law. Rather, voluntary negotiations are encouraged. It is only if an agreement cannot be reached that the regulatory body set up under the Act, the Copyright Royalty Tribunal, has the duty to determine the fee for the use in question[36].

Another example of this mechanism is found in the copyright law of Japan with respect to the broadcasting of works. Article 68 of the Japanese Copyright Act[37] provides that where a broadcasting organization requests the authorization to broadcast a work from the copyright owner and fails to reach an agreement, the work can be broadcast in any event upon the issuance of a licence by the regulatory body established under the Act and upon payment of compensation set by that regulatory body.

In both the American and Japanese examples a form of compulsory access resulted from the fact that the voluntary negotiations had failed. This is also characteristic of the compulsory licence mechanism with the exception that a round of free but unsuccessful negotiations are required before the compulsory access is triggered[38].

It is this arbitration mechanism which is used in the recently revised Australian Copyright Act to provide a special provision for the benefit of the handicapped. Pursuant to section 53D (10) of the revised Act where a work is reproduced for a handicapped user the owner of the copyright in the work reproduced may request payment. The payment is referred to as "equitable remuneration", an amount which is to be agreed upon or, in default of agreement, to be determined by a Tribunal established by the Act.

6.34 Passage of Time as a Trigger for Compulsory Access

This form of provision is somewhat unique and can be illustrated by the Japanese provisions with respect to the mechanical reproduction of musical works. Article 69 provides for both exclusive rights and compulsory access. During a three year period immediately following the sale of a commercial recording of a musical work any further recording must be based on negotiation with the owner of the copyright in the work recorded. After the expiration of the three year period a compulsory licence for recording the musical work becomes operative[39]. This type of system represents a form of compromise between the traditional exclusive rights of reproduction by recording means and the compulsory licence for mechanical reproduction for the benefit of record producers found in many jurisdictions throughout the world. It would, however, be difficult to characterize the needs of record producers as socially desirable. The purpose behind the compulsory licence for the mechanical reproduction of musical works has instead been based upon a fear of the creation of a monopoly in the recording industry.

6.35 Expropriation and Compulsory Purchases

This type of provision is found in many countries and is utilized for a variety of purposes such as cultural value and the public interest. In the Soviet Union[40], for example, the State may purchase the copyright in a published work from an author or his heirs by following a procedure set out in the laws of the Union Republics. In Nicaragua[41] when reproduction of a work is considered desirable and the owner fails to do so the Government can reproduce the work or make the right available by public auction.

6.36 Collective

The final mechanism identified is that of the collective. This mechanism does not affect either the right of authorization or remuneration. Perhaps the most important benefit of collectives is that it is a means through which compulsory licensing as a derogation from the exclusive rights of creators can be avoided:

> "Non-organized authors...constitute a growing problem which is even endangering the whole further existence of the prohibition right connected with copyright. Thus we see that in these areas (cable and reprography) the institution of legal licensing is called to help, in the United States of America in the matter of cable television, in the Netherlands for reprography, and in Germany for the public lending right[42].

Admittedly, the collective exercise of copyright rights can have certain aspects of compulsion, particularly where the activities of the collective are subject to administrative review as to royalty rates. However, an important distinction is that the creator is not forced to join the collective[43]. Rates to be charged users, by a collective, can be subject to review by some form of Tribunal or, alternatively, if agreement between users and owners cannot be reached a Tribunal can have the statutory power to fix rates. In some jurisdictions, notably the United States of America, the same Tribunal also has power to distribute royalties among rights' owners[44].

The aspect of compulsion can arise where rights' owners, through membership in a collective, cannot in certain jurisdictions refuse authorization. Such is the case in Canada, for example. The collective administers rights and licences use as often as desired, for a specified time, upon payment of a set fee. The logical extension of this is as proposed by the Whitford Committee in the United Kingdom[45]: the grant of the right would be conditional upon it being exercised collectively[46]. The various combinations and permutations of the collective exercise of copyright rights, and the limitations in the form of controls on that collective exercise, characteristically contain various forms of compulsion. Another alternative is negotiation of blanket licences using clearinghouse mechanisms with resort to anti-trust legislation in cases of abuse. The collective mechanism is used to administer the performing rights in musical works all over the world.

For purposes of general discussion six different mechanisms for the enactment of special provisions have been identified. The answer to the question of which legal mechanism is the most advantageous in meeting the needs of the production of material for the handicapped is a function of the degree of freedom or latitude provided for by the legal mechanism. The corollary of this is also true. The answer to the same question from the copyright owner's viewpoint is the legal mechanism which provides maximum control and remuneration.

An exception, as a legal mechanism, requires neither the authorization or nor payment of remuneration to the copyright owner. Thus this legal mechanism, drafted so as to blanket from copyright liability the production of material for the handicapped, gives the greatest freedom of all the mechanisms in use. In short, there is no copyright protection for the work, no permission need be sought and no payment need be tendered. At the same time the exception also represents the most serious, and therefore the least palatable, derogation from the rights of creators. A compromise between two extremes is perhaps most feasible. For example, the compulsory licence can remove one of two obstacles in the production of material for the handicapped: the need to seek out and receive authorization and the attendant time and expense of that process. The compulsory licence does not remove the other obstacle: payment of remuneration for use. On a continuum the exception represents an extreme which is located at the opposite pole from the traditional legal mechanisms of copyright law which is the provision of exclusive rights. All the other mechanisms rest on the continuum somewhere between these two extreme points. The compulsory licence, by analogy, would rest somewhere close to a mid-point on the continuum. Exclusive rights are located at one extreme and an exception at the other, and opposite, extreme.

The six legal mechanisms identified were listed merely for purposes of illustration. Many are not practical for use in meeting the requirements of the production of material for the handicapped. For example a compulsory licence or arbitration provision which is triggered by the passage of a period of time fixed by statute is not responsive to the needs of visually handicapped students who need access to material quickly. The collective mechanism may not be feasible as it does not remove the obstacle with respect to identifying whether or not a particular work is within the repertoire of the collective. This must be determined in order to decide whether individual negotiations with the copyright owner are required.

7. INTERNATIONAL ACTIVITIES

Just as some countries have enacted special provisions for the benefit of the handicapped in their copyright legislation, usually as a result of the intervention and concerted efforts of handicapped persons or agencies which represent them, so activity at the international level has been carried out within the multiplicity of international organizations and committees.

The World Council for the Welfare of the Blind (W.C.W.B.), in seeking a means of bringing certain problems to the attention of the international copyright community, was admitted as an observer in 1977 of the meetings of the Executive Committee of the Berne Union and the Intergovernmental Committee of the Universal Copyright Convention.

This action resulted in the creation of a forum through which the degree of awareness of the needs of the handicapped could be developed. This in turn led to the appointment of the W.C.W.B. to carry out a preliminary study of the question of the application of the Berne and Universal Copyright Conventions to Equipment Specially Designed for the Blind. The appointment was favourably received by numerous countries: Brazil, United States of America, Federal Republic of Germany, Austria, Israel, German Democratic Republic, Japan, France, United Kingdom, Argentina, Ghana, India, Algeria, Australia and Mauritania. Observers from international organizations such as the International Publishers Association, International Literary and Artistic Association, International Confederation of Societies of Authors and Composers and the International Writers Guild also supported the appointment.

The preliminary study was to examine the problems arising in making protected works more readily accessible to persons with handicaps and was to include a brief account of the solutions which had emerged at the national level. It was further agreed that WIPO and UNESCO should, if they considered it necessary, submit that study to a working group consisting of representatives of non-governmental organizations concerned.

The WCWB subsequently prepared a report[47]. The report centres upon the reproduction of printed works by means of raised characters, by enlarged print and by sound recordings for those unable to utilize the other means. The report characterizes access to knowledge which is contained in books and other recorded material as a fundamental need of the handicapped. The cultural and social objectives in securing this access were seen as integrating the handicapped into society and as corollaries, the achieving of independence and self-sufficiency.

The report was considered by the convention committees at their meetings in February, 1979, with a number of delegates expressing an urgent need for action:

> The delegations of Austria, Brazil, France, Germany (Federal Republic of), Ghana, Israel, Italy, Portugal, the Soviet Union, the United Kingdom, the United States of America and Yugoslavia all laid stress on the importance of such problems and on the pressing need to take whatever action was appropriate, whether legislative - if such action had not already been taken- or in the field of contracts, in order to solve those problems and facilitate the circulation of publications for the visually handicapped. Some delegations expressed the view that similar studies should be undertaken on the problems encountered in the same connection by the aurally handicapped. Some of them also thanked the delegation of Brazil for having brought the matter before the Committees at their sessions in December 1977.[48]

The proposed action was as follows:

> The Committees, each as far as it was concerned, asked their Secretariats to transmit the report prepared by the World Council for the Welfare of the Blind (W.C.W.B.) to the States party to the Berne Convention or to the Universal Copyright Convention, and also to interested international organizations. They were of the opinion that the transmittal of the report might induce the responsible authorities or the organizations of copyright owners to take appropriate action. Moreover, the States and organizations would be asked to send their comments on the report to the Secretariats. Those comments would then be evaluated by the Secretariats with the aid of a consultant and submitted to the next sessions of the Committees. Finally, the Committees expressed the desire that the problems facing the hard of hearing be investigated also[49].

Twenty countries have submitted comments on the W.C.W.B. report[50]. The Secretariat of UNESCO is analysing these comments and preparing a report which is to be included in the agenda of the next joint meeting of the Berne and Universal Copyright Convention executive committees in New Delhi in November of 1981

The nexus of domestic and international action is one which can be capitalized. Representatives of States and organizations at the international level are also influential at the national level. Ultimate change and attainment of the objective of the enactment of special provisions can only really come about by changes in domestic copyright laws. To the extent that the international scene of committees and organizations can be used to achieve the desired result it should be so utilized. At a minimum, the stated support of such organizations for the objective can do no harm.

8. INTERNATIONAL COPYRIGHT CONVENTIONS

Copyright legislation at the national level may be the most appropriate vehicle for enacting special provisions which will remove obstacles to the provision of materials for the handicapped, but national laws exist within parameters defined by the copyright conventions. Thus a substantive and political examination of the Berne and Universal Copyright Conventions will determine what action for the benefit of the handicapped is permissible, possible and practical within the Convention parameters.

8.1 Origins of the Conventions

At the international level the protection of copyright interests is secured by international agreements of which there are two of wide scope. These are the Berne Convention[7] and the Universal Copyright Convention[8]. These conventions were enacted to meet the need for a more satisfactory basis for the protection of literary and artistic works at the international level. Rather than relying on a multitude of bilateral arrangements, a multilateral agreement was created by the Berne Convention in 1886. The Universal Copyright Convention was first elaborated in 1952 for similar purposes and came into force in 1955.

The obligations of member States are determined by the text to which the State adheres. In discussing the obligations imposed by the Conventions the latest texts, revised at Paris (1971), will be used. This method has been chosen for purposes of simplification. Any action at the international level, with respect to changes in the Conventions, would be at the latest level. In addition, what will be discussed are general principles which have not varied to a great extent through the successive revisions.

In revisions of both Conventions provisions for social and cultural needs common to many member States have been made. These have been introduced for varying reasons and purposes. Special provisions, while affecting authors' rights, are deemed to be necessary to service desirable national goals and international comity.

Copyright law at the domestic level reflects a compromise between the interests of authors and the public interest as determined by particular social and cultural objectives. At the international level the factors governing domestic compromise are not operative. International compromise is reached as a result of seeking to accommodate on one hand, differing legal systems and, on the other hand, disparate social, cultural and economic needs. These differences may affect the granting and the scope of rights but, more frequently, the differences centre on the extent to which it may be possible to limit, or provide exceptions to the rights. In the main, the scope of limitations on the exclusive rights of copyright owners has been left to domestic legislations to permit national considerations to dictate peculiar needs. Thus, it has been possible at the international level to envisage permitting a range of limitations to meet the current needs of the public interest as determined at the domestic level.

8.2 The Berne Convention

The Convention has been revised a number of times, the latest text in force being that of Paris (1971). Revision of the Convention has the purpose of bringing the provisions up to date to reflect changing technology, to provide new rights, and to deal with political, economic and social change. The primary objective of the Convention is to enhance the protection afforded to literary and artistic works. This objective is subject to the recognition of the fact that encouragement of creative activity is basic to economic, cultural and social development.

In succeeding revisions, the Convention has arrived at a high degree of protection for those works which come within the ambit of the Convention. This is achieved by providing that nations subscribing to the Convention must protect works in accordance with the minimum standards provided in the text to which the member state adheres, coupled with the protection secured by national law.

The Convention, by imposing minimum protection standards, has had considerable influence on the domestic legislation in member countries. While the Convention has imposed explicit minimum protection standards with respect to the exclusive rights provided, it has not done so with regard to what can be designated as limitations on the rights of authors.

8.3 The Universal Copyright Convention

Not all countries are members of the Berne Convention for varying reasons. To provide for international relationships amongst non-Berne countries, and between Berne and non-Berne countries, the Universal Copyright Convention was elaborated in 1952. The Convention has been revised once, the latest text in force being also that of Paris (1971).

The Convention is based upon the principle of national treatment. This principle requires that each member country assimilate works protected by the Convention to domestic works by granting them the same protection granted to works of the member country's own nationals. In other words, each member country accords the protection of its national law to the works of nationals of all other contracting States. This principle applies to limitations on exclusive rights as well as to the rights granted by the domestic law.

The reasons given with respect to the objectives of revising the Berne Convention apply equally to revising the Universal Copyright Convention: to improve the protection and to reflect change.

8.4 The Availability of Various Mechanisms

A variety of legal mechanisms have been identified as being utilized by Berne and Universal Copyright Convention countries to enact what has been referred to as special provisions. These mechanisms include the exception, the compulsory licence, an arbitration provision, passage of time as a trigger for compulsory access, expropriation and the collective exercise of rights.

Those mechanisms which can be generally characterized as compelling access to copyright material will be examined together. These mechanisms are: the compulsory licence, the arbitration provision, passage of time as a trigger for compulsory access and expropriation. The common element of these four mechanisms is the removal of the right of authoriz-tion. In each case the copyright owner does not possess a right to refuse authorization to the user. The right of remuneration may or may not be present.

Finally, the mechanism which has been referred to as the "collective" exercise of rights can be summarily discussed and dismissed. The collective exercise of rights usually involves both of the traditional rights of authorization and remuneration. The individual copyright owner authorizes the collective to exercise certain rights. This is usually done by assignment of the rights in question. However, the individual copyright owner generally retains the right to refuse to join the collective. This, therefore, requires the user to first determine whether or not the collective may authorize the use requested. For the handicapped, and producers of material for them, the time, expense and refusals of permission inherent in such a system makes the collective approach to a solution undesirable. The granting of a right upon the condition that it be collectively exercised effectively removes the right of authorization from the individual copyright owner. The permissibility of such a provision under the Berne Convention is questionable. Another permutation is where the collective itself does not have a right of refusal.

The mechanisms remaining for consideration are the exception, which takes away from the copyright owner both the right of authorization and remuneration; and compulsory access which, for the purposes of this examination, is viewed as leaving the right of remuneration intact. The relevant provisions in the two copyright conventions with respect to these mechanisms give rise to different legal considerations each of which is considered separately.

8.41 The Universal Copyright Convention

Article 1 of the Universal Copyright Convention requires that each Contracting State provide "adequate and effective protection of the rights of authors and other copyright proprietors". The meaning of "adequate and effective protection" has been interpreted in various ways by the

Contracting States of the Convention. Limitations of the rights of creators also vary within the limits permitted by the Convention.

With respect to the rights protected and the permissible limitations on those rights Article IV bis explicitly provides three basic economic rights: reproduction, broadcasting and public performance. The same article also provides that domestic legislations may make "exceptions" that do not conflict with the "spirit" of the Conventions. Any State enacting such an "exception" must continue to provide "a reasonable degree of effective protection" to the rights affected.

It is within the terms of these provisions governing the protection required and the limitations permitted that the issue of both exceptions and compulsory licences for the benefit of the handicapped will be addressed. First, with respect to compulsory licences, it is impossible to render a definitive opinion on the question of whether it is permissible to introduce a scheme of compulsory licences in Universal Copyright Convention countries.

The Convention does not enumerate the works to be protected but rather utilizes the broad operative phrase "literary, scientific and artistic works". The rights attaching to those works within the ambit of the operative phrase are not detailed beyond the basic economic rights. The question of whether the limitation of rights, by a compulsory licence, is the provision of "adequate and effective protection" is open to interpretation.

There is a range of compulsory licences set out in the Convention which Contracting States may introduce into their domestic law. Article V provides for a right of translation which is, under certain specified conditions, subject to a compulsory licence. The licence permits the translation of a work into the language of the contracting state. In addition there is a range of compulsory licences available for the benefit of developing countries.

While the Universal Copyright Convention provides for these compulsory licences it by no means follows that these specific provisions allow the introduction of general compulsory licensing. Indeed, an argument based on the legal maxim of statutory interpretation that 'express mention of one person or thing is the exclusion of the other' could be made. The express mention of the possibility of compulsory licensing in the Convention in certain situations precludes the use of the mechanism in other situations:

> ...the inclusion in the Convention of special provisions allowing developing countries to publish certain works and translations under compulsory licences, means a contrario that, except as provided in Article V, there could be no question of developed countries instituting a general system of compulsory licensing for the publication of literary, scientific and artistic works[51].

This view was adopted by the revision Conference:

> The Conference adopted the principle, it being understood that a 'general system' referred either to a system applying to a specific type of work with respect to all forms of uses, or to a system applying to all types of works with respect to a particular form of use[52].

An example of the former would include a compulsory licence applying to a literary work with respect to any use, including handicapped use. An example of the latter would include a compulsory licence applicable to all works for the use of the handicapped.

The question which must be answered at the national level is whether the introduction of compulsory licensing will provide "adequate and effective protection" including whether one or more compulsory licences come within that determination[53]. Although the question is not free from doubt it is submitted that the authorities cited could support an argument that the use of the compulsory licence mechanism is precluded in Universal Copyright Convention countries except in those cases or situations where explicit provision is contained within the Convention permitting its use.

The question of "exceptions" to protection in Universal Copyright Convention countries, as an alternative to the compulsory licence mechanism, gives rise to the consideration of yet another article of the Convention. Article IV bis provides that domestic legislations may make exceptions that do not conflict with the "spirit" of the Conventions and any State enacting such exceptions must continue to provide "a reasonable degree of effective protection" to the rights affected.

As was the case with respect to the introduction of compulsory licences, it is submitted that the range of exceptions which would not conflict with the spirit of the Convention is a question of interpretation for the jurisdiction concerned. In the case at hand, the issue is whether exceptions to the rights of reproduction, performance and, in a limited sense, publication, fall within the criteria set out in Article IV bis.

Finally, it has to be emphasized that any exceptions introduced by Contracting States at the national level, under the rubric of affording a "reasonable degree of effective protection" are limited to those States, and do not apply in other Contracting States. Moreover, such exceptions would, in any event, be limited in their application to works having a Universal Copyright Convention country as the country of origin. Thus, the effects of such material exceptions is severely limited in international terms. The same situation exists with respect to relations between Berne member countries.

The fact that some Universal Copyright Convention countries are of the view that exceptions can be introduced is illustrated by the exception in the copyright law of the United States of America with respect of certain performances for the benefit of, inter alia, the handicapped[54]. It is submitted that other exceptions to other rights for the benefit of the handicapped, would be equally within the ambit of Article IV bis. The introduction of an exception for the benefit of the handicapped could arguably still leave the author or other copyright proprietor with a "reasonable degree of effective protection". This point is fully discussed below with respect to the Berne requirement of non-interference with normal exploitation.

8.42 The Berne Convention

The discussion of the availability of the exception mechanism under the Berne Convention requires the examination of two articles: Articles 9 and, by way of analogy, Article 10. Article 9, paragraph 1, provides that authors are to have the exclusive right of authorizing the reproduction of their works "in any manner or form". Paragraph 2, provides that exceptions can be made by national legislation, subject to three conditions:

1. the intervention can only go to a "special case";
2. that any authorized reproduction must not conflict with the normal exploitation of the work;
3. that the exception must not "unreasonably prejudice the legitimate interests of the author".

The designation of special cases is subject to two conditions: that there be no conflict with the normal exploitation of the particular work and that the exception must not unreasonably prejudice the legitimate interests of the author.

The Record of the Stockholm Revision Conference is instructive with respect to the working, interpretation and sequence of Article 9(2):

> If it is considered that reproduction conflicts with the normal exploitation of the work, reproduction is not permitted at all. If it is considered that reproduction does not conflict with the normal exploitation of the work, the next step would be to consider

> whether it does unreasonably prejudice the legitimate interests of the author. Only if such is not the case would it be possible in certain special cases to introduce a compulsory licence, or to provide for use without payment.[55]

The meaning of these two conditions is illustrated by an example dealing with reprography:

> A practical example might be photocopying for various purposes. If it consists of producing a very large number of copies, it may not be permitted, as it conflicts with a normal exploitation of the work. If it implies a rather large number of copies for use in industrial undertakings, it may not unreasonably prejudice the legitimate interests of the author, provided that, according to national legislation, an equitable remuneration is paid. If a small number of copies is made, photocopying may be permitted without payment, particularly for individual or scientific use.[56]

The scope of the exception in terms of "normal exploitation" is illustrated by the photocopying example. "Normal exploitation" refers to the usual means utilized to exploit the work. The exception is not permitted if it includes the usual means of exploiting the work. For example, a book is normally exploited by printing copies for sale. If the reporduction envisaged by the exception is the same as that used by the author then that process is one which conflicts with the normal exploitation of the work. Similarly, if the result of use, pursuant to the exception, was to reduce or replace the monetary returns anticipated as a result of normal exploitation, then there would also be a conflict with the rule set out in Article 9(2):

> If the contemplated reproduction would be such as to conflict with a normal exploitation of the work it is not permitted at all. Novels, schoolbooks, etc., are normally exploited by being printed and sold to the public. This Article does not permit member countries to allow this e.g. under compulsory licences, even if payment is made to the copyright owner.[57]

With respect to the condition of "not unreasonably prejudicing the legitimate interests of an author" it is clear that a "reasonable" exception is permissible. Even though any reproduction may damage the author or copyright owner to some extent, the range permitted by the Convention is a question of degree. The making of a few copies may be reasonable where the making of hundreds would not:

> If the first condition is met (the reproduction does not conflict with the normal exploitation of the work) one must look and see whether the second is satisfied. Note that it is not a question of prejudice or no: All copying is damaging in some degree: a single photocopy may mean one copy of the journal remaining unsold and, if the author had a share in the proceeds of publication he lost it. But was this prejudice unreasonable? Here, scarcely. It might be otherwise if a monograph, printed in limited numbers, were copied by a large firm and the copies distributed in their thousands to its correspondents throughout the world.[58]

It is possible to argue that the exceptions envisaged by Article 9(2) could be broadly interpreted so as to include a special provision for the benefit of the handicapped. The first of the conditions contained in Article 9(2) is that the intervention can only go to a "special case". The class of handicapped members of society represent a special case in two senses. First, the handicapped are an easily identifiable class of persons per se. Secondly, handicapped persons are not as a rule a class in respect of which there has been an identification with the routine exploitation of works.

The normal exploitation of literary works is by printing and selling to the public. With respect to the "special case" of the handicapped it is clear that the class does not come within the range of normal exploitation in that members of the class do not buy books in their original form. By admitting the visually handicapped to be a special case in respect of which there is no anticipation of normal exploitation, it follows that the provision of an exception to permit reproduction for the benefit of the handicapped would not unreasonably prejudice the legitimate interests of an author. It could also be argued that the provisions of Article 9(2) can be seen as an attempt to circumscribe direct reproduction.[59] Reproduction for handicapped users does not involve direct reproduction but rather adaptation into special media of varying kinds.

The conditions under which an exception can be enacted pursuant to Article 9(2) may be usefully contrasted with the provisions of Article 10(2) which leaves to the legislation of Union countries the freedom to permit the use of works "by way of illustration in publications, broadcasts or sound or visual recordings for teaching". This is permitted provided the use is consonant with fair practice and is justified by the purpose. It is striking that no reference is made to normal exploitation, nor to unreasonably prejudicing the legitimate interests of the author. Much more leeway appears to be available to legislators to enact legislation which meets the perceived needs of domestic interests in furthering education. With respect to Article 10(2) which permits use of a work for teaching purposes, the very centre of W.C.W.B.'s concerns, national legislation is permitted a much wider scope to enact laws which would meet the purpose envisaged. The educational needs of the handicapped clearly fall within the wide ambit of this provision.

There are numerous and varying instances in national legislations where exceptions to the rights of authors have been provided. In a significant number of cases it is problematical that the exceptions come within those envisaged by the convention. The latitude permitted by Article 9 has been widely interpreted by Union countries. The question of possible strict technical compliance has been overcome by many Union countries for a variety of purposes, including in some countries the purpose of benefitting the handicapped. This, in the final analysis, may prove to be the most persuasive and practical evidence in support of international action. In many countries uses or borrowings of a nature not comtemplated by the Convention have been introduced. These include library use, use by agricultural fairs, educational, religious and personal use. These illustrate the latitude member countries have exercised within their obligations under the Convention.

The discussion thus far has dealt with an exception to the right of reproduction. Exceptions to the rights of performance and publication should also be examined as these were also affected by the special provisions identified as being for the benefit of the handicapped. Discussion of the exception with respect to performance rights was prompted by the provisions of the United States of America's copyright law which exempted certain performances from copyright liability when they were intended for the handicapped. This type of service to the handicapped is also carried out by broadcasting methods such as special media broadcasts substituting for print the reading of printed materials. The signal's receipt may be restricted to the handicapped or be generally receivable. Thus, the availability of an exception to the broadcasting right should also be examined.

The Convention provides for the right of public performance in Article 11 and the right of public recitation in Article 11ter. These two rights are subsumed under the rubric of the public performance right in most national laws with the right attaching to all works. The two rights together require protection against the public performance of a work, which effectively covers all communication except for broadcasting which is also an exclusive right of the copyright owner under Article 11 bis. The provision of various reading services, whether live or by broadcast, involves all of these rights in one form or another.

No express mention of the possibility of limiting these rights by means of an exception is made in the Convention except the possibility of compulsory access with respect to the broadcasting of works. The possibility of acquiring compulsory access to permit the broadcasting of works for the benefit of the handicapped would be subject to the condition that negotiation must first be entered into. It is only after negotiations have failed that the possibility of compulsory access arises. This is what has been referred to as the arbitration mechanism. The legal issues arising here are complex but, in general, the Convention does permit what are called "minor reservations". The broad umbrella of this phrase is considered to cover such diverse activities as performances at religious ceremonies and public holidays. Limitations which are "minor" are considered permissible with respect to both public performance and broadcasting rights and have been broadly interpreted, without apparent repercussion in a number of countries. The provision of reading services specifically designed for the handicapped could arguably fall within the broad ambit of the "minor reservations" umbrella. The substantive legal issues would be best addressed, however, based upon a detailed draft provision and an exact opinion sought as to its compliance with the terms of the Convention.

With respect to an exception to the right of publication it will be recalled that those Berne and Universal Copyright Convention countries with special provisions for the benefit of the handicapped apply those provisions to published works only. The right of publication was affected only in a secondary way, in that the publication was of an adapted version of an already published work.

The Convention does not specifically deal with this form of limitation. However, an examination of the traditional rationale of the right of publication may be valuable in discussing whether a limitation of the right is permissible.

The origins of the right of publication are based on notions of a creator's right to decide whether or not to disclose his work to the public. In the special provisions for the benefit of the handicapped identified this initial disclosure has already been made as only published works are brought within the special provision. On this basis it could be argued that any limitation on the right to publish, in the limited sense of publication in a special medium intended specifically for the handicapped, is not a fundamental but rather a minor, and therefore permissible limitation, which does not affect or limit the exercise of the exclusive right to publish but only assists in making an already published work available to the handicapped.

The discussion thus far has dealt with the legal mechanism of the exception. What follows is a discussion of the availability of the compulsory licence mechanism in Berne Convention countries. The Convention contains provisions which envisage the possibility of three different compulsory licences being enacted in domestic legislation. The first is with respect to the grant of a broadcasting right which is coupled with a provision to permit the compulsion of broadcasting of a work[60]. The rationale of the licence is that broadcasting involves the public interest as it serves the cultural and social interests of the public. It was argued that author's rights should not override that public interest, particularly with regard to using broadcasting as a means of education and the furtherance of culture. The licence may not prejudice the moral rights of the author nor his right to obtain equitable remuneration.

The second compulsory licence is for the benefit of sound recording producers[61]. This compulsory licence emerged from the debate between composers wishing to secure the exclusive right of authorizing the recording of their musical works on one hand, and the recording industry, on the other hand, which had sprung up as a result of the new reproduction technology. It was feared the granting of exclusive rights to composers would create a monopoly situation which would operate to the detriment of the infant recording industries. The mechanism to reconcile the opposing views was that of the establishment of the possibility of a compulsory licence system whereby manufacturers of recordings were required to pay royalties to composers but did not require the composer's authorization to make the recording.

The third group of licences was first adopted in 1967 but never came into force. However, the "Special Provisions for Developing Countries" which are introduced in Article 21 and set out in an Appendix, became an integral part of the 1971 text. The Appendix, in sum, makes it possible for developing countries, to introduce non-exclusive, non-assignable compulsory licences to translate and/or reproduce protected works used for instructional purposes and for teaching, scholarship or research.

Authorities previously cited were of the view that the provisions of Article 9(2) extended not only to free use in the form of exceptions but also to compulsory licences:

> If it is considered that reproduction conflicts with the normal exploitation of the work reproduction is not permitted at all. If it is considered that reproduction does not conflict with the normal exploitation of the work, the next step would be to consider whether it does not unreasonably prejudice the legitimate interests of the author. Only if such is not the case would it be possible in certain special cases to introduce a compulsory licence, or to provide use without payment.[62]

An argument in support of this position is that the compulsory licence is a less serious derogation from author's rights than an exception. The compulsory licence takes away the right of authorization whereas the exception takes away the right of remuneration as well as the right of authorization. If the more serious derogation in the form of an exception is permissible under the Convention then the less serious, the compulsory licence, must also be permitted.

This view is not universally held however. The arguments in support of the propositon that compulsory licences cannot be enacted in domestic legislation unless the Convention expressly so permits is based upon interpretation of the Convention. By providing for the possibility of only certain licences the Convention precludes the possibility of others. The maxim expressio unius personal vei rei, est exclusio alterius, the express mention of one person or thing is the exclusion of the other, is a rule used in construing laws and documents. Applying the rule it can be argued that the only possibility of introducing compulsory licences is with respect to those set out in the Convention. Thus the subjection of literary works to a compulsory licence is prohibited.

Any Berne Union country may grant protection in excess of the minimum standards guaranteed by the Convention. However "the opposite would be against the fundamental intention of the Convention"[63]. Any reduction of the minimum standards is prohibited. As compulsory licences are a limitation on exclusive rights, to provide compulsory licences not envisaged by the Convention could be considered uncontemplated limitations rendering protection below the minimum standards required.

The substantive issues involved in the question of whether the compulsory licence mechanism is available for use in dealing with the needs of the handicapped are highly technical. The preceding discussion is merely a cursory examination of the difficult legal issues involved. The availability of the compulsory licence as a mechanism is at best uncertain. Detailed and sophisticated legal arguments are outside the scope of the present study. Such a study however would be valuable as the compulsory licence, if available, could provide an ideal compromise of the interests involved thereby facilitating concrete action.

Final determination of the availability of the compulsory licence mechanism in Berne countries must rest with the appropriate governing body of the Convention itself. For the purposes of production of material for the handicapped the compulsory licence mechanism does present a practical solution as obstacles to access are effectively removed. To opt for this mechanism, despite its uncertain availability, may lead to a time consuming and therefore delaying legal debate. In addition, the compulsory licence mechanism will require payment for the privilege of using works protected by copyright. Also, the compulsory licence is not a device that is generally accepted at the international level. While the mechanism is a feature of Anglo-American law it is not, for instance, acceptable in French law. On the positive side the compulsory licence is a more palatable mechanism from the copyright owners point of view as it takes away only one of the two traditional copyright rights.

8.5 Summary

The Conventions set out the legal obligations of member countries. Those obligations are variously interpreted by those member countries. Some have interpreted their obligations to permit special provisions for the handicapped without any apparent repercussions. The special provisions currently in use utilize a variety of legal mechanisms but for the special needs of the handicapped either the exception or the compulsory licence provides the most practical solution. It appears that a sound legal argument can be made for the introduction of the exception, as a legal mechanism, in both Berne and Universal Copyright Convention countries. However, the availability of the compulsory licence mechanism is uncertain. Some Berne and Universal Copyright Convention countries[64] have introduced compulsory licences for the production of talking books without any apparent repercussion but that does not necessarily mean that the use of the mechanism is permitted in a strict legal sense.

8.6 Political Considerations

The ideal solution to the problems of the handicapped, and of producers of material for that group, with respect to access barriers created by copyright legislation, is the enactment of special provisions for their benefit in domestic copyright legislation. At the international level recognition of the ideal solution would be that of revising the conventions to provide specifically for a special provision for the benefit of the handicapped. To have the Conventions so revised for that purpose alone is most unlikely. Revision conferences are held at the instance of member States to deal with matters which, in general, have been the subject of investigation by groups of experts or sub-committees. Calls for revision are, in the usual course, expressed by the committees of the Conventions.

Proposals for revision are seldom the result of one meeting or at the urging of one government. Rather, proposals result from a fusion of efforts taking place over several years in numerous meetings of various groups. At such meetings compromises are worked out, and it is those compromises which are considered as revision proposals. As such, the proposal has a degree of acceptance and adoption is likely.

Revision conferences require considerable preparatory work, cost large amounts of money and, normally, are held only when the direct interests of States are involved. To envisage a revision conference is unrealistic if it were to be held for the single purpose of providing exceptions for the handicapped. Alternatively, it would be more realistic to foresee the inclusion in a revision conference, held for other purposes, of a consideration of proposals advanced to benefit the handicapped community. At the present time there are no apparent initiatives being taken to arrange for a revision conference in the foreseeable future. Putting aside the possibility of revision it is possible to envisage the taking of other steps. The Report prepared by the W.C.W.B. was circulated to member States of both the Berne and Universal Copyright Convention in the hope it "might induce the responsible authorities or the organizations of copyright owners to take appropriate action". This action will include consideration of the issue at the next joint meeting of the committees at New Delhi in November of 1981.

Such action could also include the formation of a group of experts composed of representatives of governments members of the committees and observer organizations such as the W.C.W.B. and IFLA to identify and consider both the problems and possible solutions. The group could be constituted as a joint sub-committee of the Committees with a mandate to issue a report in respect of which subsequent action would be considered by the Committees. It is of course essential that this sub-committee, have before it a working paper for consideration. This paper would need to be prepared by or for IFLA and the W.C.W.B. and should, <u>inter alia</u>, set forth positions, requirements and other relevant material.

The objectives of the sub-committee should be, <u>inter alia</u>, to recommend action to enable the Committees to decide upon a resolution advising member States of the problems, identifying possible solutions, and advocating the adoption of certain provisions at the national level. Such a resolution would not have any legal effect. Its effect would be only moral, but at a minimum it may lead to the providing of exceptions at present. At a maximum, the resolution could lead to much greater recognition of the problems.

Both the Berne and Universal Copyright Convention Committees, in exercising their mandates, are free to bring to the attention of member States the resolutions they adopt. The Berne Executive Committee resolution would be the final step in respect of particular action. However, with regard to the Universal Copyright Convention Intergovernmental Committee, there is a further step which could be taken, but only following upon the Committee adopting their own resolution.

The Universal Copyright Convention is an international instrument coming under the aegis of Unesco, and the pursuit and advancement of international copyright is a function, inter alia, of the Communications and Culture program of Unesco. Unesco meets in General Conference every two years to consider the program and budget of the organization. During the Conference proceedings various resolutions are advanced by member States and may be adopted by the Conference as a whole. Resolutions which deal with exhorting member States to adopt certain positions are not binding but have a certain measure of moral suasion.

It would be entirely appropriate for IFLA and W.C.W.B. to initiate proposals advocating the putting forward a draft resolution for adoption by the General Conference. Such a resolution would identify the problem, and urge the necessity of adopting solutions. It could advocate particular solutions and be couched in terms of the General Conference calling upon Member States to adopt measures to solve the problems.

SUMMARY AND RECOMMENDATIONS

The provision of library services to handicapped readers presents unique characteristics, a major one being that libraries must often produce the special format materials required by their handicapped readers. Thus the normally clear line between publisher and librarian is blurred as librarians become involved in original transcription and production of materials in special formats.

Improved production and dissemination of materials for the handicapped, while providing better services to readers, have brought forward copyright problems which can result in barriers to the production and dissemination of materials in special formats. Copyright problems can occur when an original transcription is made from the printed edition of a published work into a special format for handicapped readers, or when additional copies are required to serve readers outside the jurisdiction for which the original permission was granted.

The appropriate method of resolving problems caused by copyright laws is to change the laws, in order to remove these legislative barriers or to provide special benefits for handicapped readers.

Few countries have enacted special provisions for the handicapped in their copyright laws. Those special provisions which do exist differ greatly in the activities which they cover, the rights which they affect, and the conditions within which they operate.

A significantly larger number of countries have enacted special provisions for other socially desirable purposes, such as education. These special provisions provide a precedent for the enactment of special provisions for the handicapped, which also fall within the broad ambit of socially desirable purposes.

The major impetus for legislative change will need to come from within each country, but activity at the international level is also being carried out: The World Council for the Welfare of the Blind has been particularly successful in bringing copyright problems to the attention of the international copyright community.

The protection of copyright interests functions internationally through the Berne Convention and the Universal Copyright Convention, which impose certain parameters which must be respected by member countries. The ideal international solutions to copyright problems is to revise the conventions to provide special provisions for the handicapped. Alternative action includes working toward the adoption of a resolution by UNESCO which would request member states to adopt certain measures to resolve copyright problems.

The recommendations which follow are derived from positions outlined in this study. Most are intended for IFLA action, on the double premise that IFLA is an association which must advocate better library services for everyone, including the handicapped, and that IFLA is a central point from which proposals for action can emanate and be directed either to appropriate international agencies, or to its own member associations and institutions.

9.1 General Recommendations

The following recommendations, although not directly related to copyright, are viewed as direct and positive steps which IFLA can take to assist in creating a more productive environment for the development of library services for the handicapped. They should be undertaken coincidentally with other more specific actions to resolve copyright problems. Indeed, unless bibliographic controls are strengthened and linked, and unless interlibrary loan, exchange, sales and import/export agreements are implemented on a wider and more consistent scale, the ultimate benefit of activities to resolve copyright problems would be diminished.

9.11 Number of Handicapped Persons

In the International Year of Disabled Persons, it is unfortunate to note that there is no concrete estimate of the number of persons unable to read print because of a physical handicap. IFLA should consider an approach to the United Nations, and in particular the World Health Organization and UNESCO, to request that a study be conducted to determine the number of persons unable to read print because of a physical handicap, and to analyse and categorize the causes of such handicaps.

9.12 Definition of Handicapped

IFLA should recommend to its members that the expression "unable to read print because of a physical handicap" be preferred to the normally used word "blind" when referring to persons whose physical handicaps prevent them from reading print. The legal definition of "blindness" which exists in many countries, although useful for certain purposes, is misleading and limiting when applied to persons who require the use of special format materials, the group with which IFLA is concerned. Where a more detailed explanation of the expression "unable to read print because of a physical handicap" is required, the following categories can be used:

> Persons unable to read print because of a physical handicap include those who may have a visual impairment, e.g. who are totally without sight, or whose visual impairment, with correction and regardless of optical measurement, prevents the reading of standard printed material; Motor impairment, e.g. who are physically impaired to the extent that they are incapable of reading standard print or holding a book or turning its pages. This includes persons who have paralysis, muscular dystrophy, cerebral palsy or other motor disabilities of a temporary or permanent nature; Neurological impairment, e.g. who have a neurological dysfunction of an organic or functional nature which results in an inability to interpret or understand printed words or sentences.

9.13 Universal Availability of Publications

IFLA should recognize and work to ensure that special format materials currently available be made available throughout the world via interlibrary loan, exchange, sales, import/export and duplication agreements. It should request of agencies producing materials for the handicapped that their original transcription or master copy of a work transcribed from print into another medium for the handicapped be considered a world resource.

Such a recommendation places a heavy burden of responsibility on the original transcribing agency which must then be prepared to made available sub-masters or other copies of its transcriptions to other agencies serving handicapped readers. By such a recommendation, IFLA would begin to eliminate "limited distribution" services, which result in wasteful duplication of original transcription, and which further fragment an already overly fragmented service.

9.14 National Union Catalogues

IFLA should recommend that national libraries establish or sponsor the establishment of a national union catalogue of special format materials for handicapped readers, as is presently the case in the U.S.A. and Australia. The data contained therein should be widely available, preferably as a component of the MARC network, to facilitate international access to material for the handicapped.

The concepts of Universal Bibliographic Control and Universal Availability of Publications take on an added and more urgent dimension when applied to the provision of special format materials for the handicapped, because the pool of transcribed materials is so small, and the need to share them so great.

9.2 Copyright Recommendations

9.21 Right of Access to Published Information

Countries hold specific views on where the production and dissemination of materials for the handicapped fit within the broad spectrum of their copyright philosophy. In some cases, the view might be held that a handicapped persons's right of access to information is paramount, and that certain derogations from the rights of authors are required for the greater good of society.

Other countries might believe just as strongly that author's rights are paramount, and that no major derogation from those rights should be enacted on behalf of the handicapped.

In many jurisdictions today, the possibility exists for copyright owners to refuse permission for the transcription of a published work into another medium for use by a handicapped person, thus denying that reader access to published information solely by reason of his handicap. Such a possibility cannot be tolerated in any society dedicated to the principle of freedom of access to information.

In order to assure everyone an equal right of access to information, one of the basic rights of a copyright owner, the right to authorize, needs to be derogated to some extent. IFLA must give serious consideration to the principle that a copyright owner should not have the right to refuse permission for a published work to be transcribed into another format for use by a person unable to read the printed edition because of a physical handicap.

The Right to Remuneration

In several countries, notably Denmark, Australia and Norway, remuneration or compensation is paid to the copyright owner when published works are transcribed into another medium for the handicapped. Remuneration is not required by law in several other countries, including Japan, Sweden and Finland. It would therefore be inappropriate for IFLA to make a general recommendation in this matter, which is a subjective issue related to the philosophical approach of a country toward the needs of its society as a whole, weighed against the copyright proprietor's interests. If requested to state an opinion, IFLA might consider the position that it does not object to remuneration on principle if producing agencies and copyright owners are in agreement over the proposed payment system in that country.

9.23 Other Considerations

In examining current laws which have enacted special provisions for the handicapped, it is possible to identify certain factors which are deserving of support in principle.

The first concerns who may benefit from special provisions while transcribing a work into a special format for the handicapped. The least restrictive option as seen in Sweden, is that anyone, including a commercial enterprise, may benefit providing that a handicapped person is the ultimate user.

Another factor concerns works which may be subject to the special provisions. In all countries which have enacted special provisions for the handicapped, only published works are subject to the provisions. The arguments for this are reasonable, and are worthy of support in principle.

A third factor concerns the definition of the ultimate user for which provisions were intended. The least restrictive option is to be preferred, in this case the group of readers referred to throughout this study as being "unable to read printed materials because of a physical handicap".

A final factor concerns use of the specially transcribed published material. Again, the least restrictive view is preferred, which includes the loan and/or sale of materials to serve educational, informational and cultural needs of handicapped readers.

9.24 Increasing Awareness of Copyright Problems

It is sad to note that so few countries have enacted special copyright provisions for the benefit of the handicapped. This is due in part to the fact that there is little public awareness of copyright problems which create barriers to the production and dissemination of material for the handicapped. IFLA can be useful in acting as a forum for discussion in this area, to increase awareness of problems and their possible solutions, and to educate IFLA members about the role which they can play in fostering positive action in their respective jurisdictions.

9.3 Recommendations for International Action

While urging its members to work at their own national level to enact copyright legislation which is favourable to the provision and dissemination of library materials for the handicapped, IFLA might consider further action to carry on the work begun by W.C.W.B. to influence the international copyright community.

9.31 Agreement on Copyright Law Principles

Although this study recommends that IFLA support in principle certain positions vis-à-vis copyright and materials for the handicapped, there is no recommendation for a specific formula or model copyright provision. The absence of a recommended formula results from a lack of consensus in this matter among those involved in the production and dissemination of materials for the handicapped. The lack of a unified voice from the library sector can only delay action at all levels, and give an advantage to those who would oppose special provisions for the handicapped in copyright laws. It is therefore suggested that IFLA convene a meeting with representatives of W.C.W.B. to consider and resolve the following questions:

(a) What services for handicapped users should be brought within the terms of a model special provision enacted into national copyright laws?

(b) Which of the copyright rights should be limited by a model special provision?

(c) Who would be permitted to act with impunity under the special provision?

(d) Which works protected by copyright would be brought within the ambit of the special provision?

(e) What conditions precedent to the operation of the special provision would be required?

(f) Would remuneration be required and, if so, by whom should it be paid?

(g) Which legal mechanism should be used?

The aim of this meeting would be to arrive at a consensus within the library community, and to develop strategies for future action, notably in IFLA/W.C.W.B. dealings with Unesco, the Copyright Conventions, and international publisher's and author's associations.

The second aim, if time permits, would be the preparation of a working paper setting out the consensus position of W.C.W.B. and IFLA, together with reasons in support thereof, for submission to the joint meeting of the committees of the Berne and Universal Copyright Conventions in New Delhi in November of 1981.

9.32 Support of Allied Industries

When a unified position on copyright matters has been arrived at by IFLA and W.C.W.B., IFLA should inform international author and publisher organizations of its activities in this field, and attempt to obtain their support.

IFLA can and must play a leading role in fostering action to resolve copyright problems in relation to library materials for the handicapped readers. The range of possible actions is wide, going from the sponsorship of discussions to create an awareness of the special needs of handicapped readers, to the exhortation of IFLA members to pursue specific objectives in attempting to influence national copyright legislation, to the more complex and long-term involvement in international copyright conventions. Each course of action will bring its own rewards, and each will be a contribution to a greater ideal, that of a society which recognizes the needs of all of its citizens for access to information, and accepts the responsibility of serving those needs.

REFERENCES

1. American Foundation for the Blind. Reading with Print Limitations, Executive Summary. Findings from: A Survey to Determine the Extent of the Eligible User Population Not Currently Being Served or Not Aware of the Programs of the Library of Congress National Library Service for the Blind and Physically Handicapped. Prepared for the Library of Congress National Library Service for the Blind and Physically Handicapped. New York, 1979. p.18.

2. World Bank. World Development Report. Washington, 1980. Table 47, p. 142-143.

3. Canadian National Institute for the Blind. Statistical Studies on the Blind Population of Canada Registered with CNIB, 1979. Toronto, 1980. (Pamphlet).

4. French, Richard Slayton. From Homer to Helen Keller, a social and educational study of the blind. New York, American Foundation for the Blind, 1932. p. 41.

5. Schauder, D. E. and M. D. Cram. Libraries for the Blind - An international study of policies and practices. Steverage, England, Peter Peregrinus, 1977. (Librarianship and Information Studies, Volume 4). p. 10.

6. The identification of these countries is based on a World Intellectual Property Organization publication entitled Copyright Law Survey, Geneva, 1979. This consists of seventy three countries: Algeria, Argentina, Australia, Austria, Bangladesh, Belgium, Brazil, Bulgaria, Canada, Chile, Colombia, Costa Rica, Cuba, Cyprus, Czechoslovakia, Denmark, Ecuador, Egypt, El Salvador, Finland, France, German Democratic Republic, Germany (Federal Republic of), Ghana, Greece, Guatemala, Haiti, Hungary, Iceland, India, Ireland, Italy, Ivory Coast, Japan, Kenya, Lebanon, Liberia, Libyan Arab Jamahiriya, Liechtenstein, Luxembourg, Malawi, Malta, Mexico, Monaco, Morocco, Netherlands, New Zealand, Nicaragua, Nigeria, Norway, Pakistan, Panama, Paraguay, Peru, Philippines, Poland, Portugal, Romania, Senegal, South Africa, Soviet Union, Spain, Sweden, Switzerland, Thailand, Tunisia, Turkey, United Kingdom, United States of America, Uruguay, Venezuela, Yugoslavia, Zambia.

7. Berne Convention for the Protection of Literary and Artistic Works 1886, as amended at Berlin (1908), Rome (1928), Brussels (1948), Stockholm (1967) and Paris (1971).

8. Geneva (1952), as amended at Paris (1971).

9. Copyright Law, No. 48, of May 6, 1970, Article 37.

10. Act No. 158 on Copyright in Literary and Artistic Works, of May 31, 1961, Article 18.

11. Law No. 404, Relating to Copyright in Literary and Artistic Works, of July 8, 1961, Article 18.

12. Copyright Act, of May 29, 1972, Article 19.

13. Act Relating to Property Rights in Literary, Scientific or Artistic Works, No. 2 of May 12, 1961, Article 17.

14. Fundamentals of Civil Legislation of the Union of Soviet Socialist Republics and the Union Republics of December 8, 1961; in particular Chapter IV on Copyright, Article 103(8).

15. Law No. 729, of December 30, 1960, on Copyright in Literary and Artistic Works, Article 18.

16. Copyright Act 17 U.S.C., Public Law 94-553, of October 19, 1976, subsections 110(2), (8) and (9) and section 710 together with the regulations thereunder (Volume 45, No. 41 of the Federal Register February 28, 1980 at 13072-13074) which is not a special provision but rather provides for the creation of a voluntary licensing system tied to registration.

17. Copyright Act of May 29, 1972, Article 19.

18. Fundamentals of Civil Legislation of the Union of Soviet Socialist Republics and the Union Republics of December 8, 1961; in particular, Chapter IV on Copyright, Article 103(8).

19. Article 3, paragraph (3) of the Berne Convention, Paris text, defines published works as follows: The expression "published works" means works published with the consent of their authors, whatever may be the means of manufacture of the copies, provided that the availability of such copies has been such as to satisfy the reasonable requirements of the public, having regard to the nature of the work. The performance of a dramatic, dramatico-musical, cinematographic or musical work, the public recitation of a literary work, the communication by wire or the broadcasting of literary or artistic works, the exhibition of a work of art and the construction of a work of architecture shall not constitute publication.

    Article VI of the 1971 text of the UCC defines publication as follows: 'Publication', as used in this Convention, means the reproduction in tangible form and the general distribution to the public of copies of a work from which it can be read or otherwise visually perceived.

20. An Act for the general revision of the Copyright Law, title 17 of the United States Code, and for other purposes (Public Law 94-553), of October 19, 1976, section 110, subsections 2, 8 and 9. The United States' law draws a fine distinction between displays of certain works and performance of other works. Generally the distinction lies in the nature of the work. A literary or musical work is performed whereas an artistic work can usually only be displayed. For sake of simplicity this will hereinafter be referred to generically as the right of performance.

21. The only exception is the law of the United States of America which does not contain a special provision dealing with the right of reproduction.

22. Law for the protection of copyright and other rights connected with the exercise thereof, No. 633, of April 22, 1941, Article 68.

23. Law Relating to Literary and Artistic Property, No. 66-12, of February 14, 1966, Article 11.

24. An Act Respecting Copyright, of June 4, 1921, subparagraph 17(2)(g).

25. The Copyright Ordinance, 1962, of June 2, 1962, subsection 10(2A).

26. Federal Act on Copyright in Works of Literature and Art and on Related Rights (Copyright Act), of April 9, 1936, Article 51.

27. Law on Copyright, No. 14, of December 28, 1977.

28. Law No. 404, relating to Copyright in Literary and Artistic Works, of July 8, 1961, Article 20.

29. Copyright Law, of March 30, 1978, Article 50.

30. Law Relating to the Protection of Copyright, No. 354, of June 24, 1954, Article 12.

31. Stephen P. Ladas, The International Protection of Literary and Artistic Property, Volume 1, "International Copyright and Inter-American Copyright", New York, 1938 at 2.

32. Ladas, supra at 2.

33. This leaves aside the question of personal or moral rights which, under some theories, are regarded as an integral part of copyright. The monistic and dualistic theories of copyright are examples of this type of approach.

34. Subject to the relevant international copyright conventions.

35. What is referred to as a 'compulsory licence' also includes a legal licence. In both instances authorization is not required.

36. A. Latman, The copyright Law, 5th ed. (Washington, 1979) at 201.

37. The Copyright Law, No. 48, of May 6, 1970.

38. Time can also be yet another trigger which can change the kind of compulsory access provided for. Mechanisms 6.33 and 6.34 are variations of a compulsory licence but the triggers for each differ: Failure to reach an agreement in 6.33, passage of time in 6.34, and in 6.32 the statutory creation of a compulsory licence without any trigger or point of departure as for example for the special purpose of use by the handicapped.

39. This too is subject to a previous request for authorization and a failure to reach an agreement.

40. Fundamentals of Civil Legislation of the Union of Soviet Socialist Republics and the Union Republics of December 8, 1961; in particular Chapter IV on Copyright, Article 106.

41. Civil Code, Part IV, Articles 724-867, of February 1, 1904, Article 860.

42. The Authors Place in Society and Legal Relations Between Authors and Those Responsible for Distributing Their Works, Herman Cohen Jehoram, Copyright, November, 1978, 385, at 390.

43. An exception would occur in the United Kingdom if the Whitford proposals are implemented with respect to such activities as audio visual recording. See Copyright and Designs Law: Report of the Committee to Consider the Law on Copyright and Designs, March 1977 at 75 et seq.

44. Copyright Act 1976, Title 17 USC, Section 111, for example, provides for distribution of royalties for cable use under the direction of the Copyright Royalty Tribunal but provides no guidelines as to how to allocate the revenue as between the claimants. This has presented great problems not yet resolved. Prior to the enactment of the new law it was pointed out that: "A compulsory licence

provision has to be used in a very guarded fashion, that is, only when it is absolutely necessary...when you try to fix a total rate for all works used, you face all the problems of distribution, which in some cases may be insurmountable." Hearings on S. 1106 Before the Sub-committee on Patents, Trademarks, and Copyrights of the Committee on the Judiciary, United States Senate, 89th Cong., 2nd Sess., 12 (1966).

45. With respect to reprography and audio and visual recording.

46. In Canada the national library association has agreed to a collective to solve photocopying problems but has also stated that if collectives are not formed an exemption for library photocopying should be provided in the new Act.

47. Unesco Document B/EC/XlV/14-1GC (1971)/111/16: "Evaluation of the present situation of the problems caused by the International Copyright Legislation in the production and distribution of publications in raised characters, large type print, recorded form and radio broadcasts for the blind and visually handicapped" prepared by the World Council for the Welfare of the Blind.

48. Copyright, March, 1979 at 87. See also Copyright, March 1980 at 115.

49. Ibid.

50. Dorina de Gouvêa Nowill, Report on W.C.W.B. Activities Providing for the International Copyright Regulation of Materials Specially Intended for the Blind and Visually Handicapped. p. 5.

51. Paragraph 83 of the Intergovernmental Copyright Committee Report accompanying the IGCC text (UCC/4, Annex lX, p.9).

52. Records of the Conference for Revision of the Universal Copyright Convention, Unesco House, Paris, July 5- 24, 1971 at 67.

53. See A. Bogsch, The Law of Copyright Under the Universal Copyright Convention, 3rd ed. at 6.

54. An Act for the General Revision of the Copyright Law, title 17 of the United States Code, and for other purposes (Public Law 94-553) of October 19, 1976, section 110.

55. Stockholm Revision Conference Records at 1145-46.

56. Id.

57. Guide to the Berne Convention, WIPO, 1978 at 55. The Guide is not authoritative with respect to interpreting the Convention as "it is for the authorities concerned... to form their own opinions" Id. at 4.

58. Id. at 55.

59. Id. Explanation of the article's meaning characteristically use reprography as an example. See for example, The Guide to the Berne Convention, supra at 55.

60. Article 11 bis.

61. Article 13(1).

62. Stockholm Revision Conference Records, 11 at 1145-46. See also Guide to the Berne Convention, supra at 55.

63. S.P. Ladas, The International Protection of Literary and Artistic Property, Vol. 1,p. 189.

64. Denmark, Act. No. 158 on Copyright in Literary and Artistic Works, of May 31, 1961, Article 18 and Norway, Act Relating to Property Rights in Literary, Scientific or Artistic Works, No. 2 of May 12, 1961, Article 17.

APPENDIX "A"

Japan:

Reproduction in Braille, etc.

Article 37. (1) It shall be permissible to reproduce in Braille for the blind a work already made public.
(2) For Braille libraries and other establishments for the promotion of the welfare of the blind, designated by Cabinet Order, it shall be permissible to make recordings of a work already made public exclusively for the purpose of lending such recordings for the use of the blind.

Denmark:

18. Copies in braille may be produced of published literary or musical works. Copies of these works may likewise be photographed for educational use in schools for the deaf and sufferers from speech impediments.

For loan to the blind, sufferers from defective vision, and others unable to read ordinary books due to their disability, it is permitted to make sound recordings of published literary works, when this is not done for commercial purposes. The author shall be entitled to remuneration for such recordings.

Finland:

Article 18. A published literary or musical work may be reproduced in copies printed in braille and, by means of the fixation of sound, for use by lending libraries for blind persons.

Iceland:

Article 19. Copies in braille may be printed and published of published literary or musical works. These works may likewise be photographed for educational use in schools for the deaf and sufferers from speech impediments.

Norway:

17. Copies of a published literary or scientific work or of a musical work may be reproduced in braille. Copies of such works may also be photographed for use in education of the deaf or of persons with impedimented speech, unless a particular copy has been produced especially for such use.

The King may provide that certain specified organizations or libraries may on stipulated terms, for the purpose of gratis loans to blind or disabled persons, make recordings of published literary or scientific works on instruments which can reproduce them. The author of the work shall be entitled to compensation which shall be defrayed by the State.

Soviet Union:

Article 103. Use of a Work Without the Consent of the Author and Without the Payment of Remuneration.

Permitted without the consent of the author and without the payment of royalties, but with an obligatory indication of the name of the author whose work is used and the source of the borrowing, are:

(8) The publication in Braille for the blind of published works.

Sweden:

18. A published literary or musical work may be reproduced in copies printed in braille.

By permission of the King in Council, and according to conditions stated therein, libraries and organizations may make sound recordings of published literary works to be used for loans to blind and other seriously disabled persons.

United States of America:

110. Notwithstanding the provisions of section 106, the following are not infringements of copyright:

(2) performance of a nondramatic literary or musical work or display of a work, by or in the course of a transmission, if —

(A) the performance or display is a regular part of the systematic instructional activities of a governmental body or a nonprofit educational institution; and

(B) the performance or display is directly related and of material assistance to the teaching content of the transmission; and

(C) the transmission is made primarily for —

(i) reception in classrooms or similar places normally devoted to instruction, or

(ii) reception by persons to whom the transmission is directed because their disabilities or other special circumstances prevent their attendance in classrooms or similar places normally devoted to instruction, or

(iii) reception by officers or employees of governmental bodies as a part of their official duties or employment;

(8) performance of a nondramatic literary work, by or in the course of a transmission specifically designed for and primarily directed to blind or other handicapped persons who are unable to read normal printed material as a result of their handicap, or deaf or other handicapped persons who are unable to hear the aural signals accompanying a transmission of visual signals, if the performance is made without any purpose of direct or indirect commercial advantage and its transmission is made through the facilities of: (i) a governmental body; or (ii) a noncommercial educational broadcast station (as defined in section 397 of title

47); or (iii) a radio subcarrier authorization (as defined in 47 CFR 73.293-73.295 and 73.593-73.595); or (iv) a cable system (as defined in section 111(f)).

(9) performance on a single occasion of a dramatic literary work published at least ten years before the date of the performance, by or in the course of a transmission specifically designed for and primarily directed to blind or other handicapped persons who are unable to read normal printed material as a result of their handicap, if the performance is made without any purpose of direct or indirect commercial advantage and its transmission is made through the facilities of a radio subcarrier authorization referred to in clause (8)(iii), Provided, That the provisions of this clause shall not be applicable to more than one performance of the same work by the same performers or under the auspices of the same organization.

710. Reproduction for use of the blind and physically handicapped: Voluntary licensing forms and procedures

The Register of Copyrights shall, after consultation with the Chief of the Division for the Blind and Physically Handicapped and other appropriate officials of the Library of Congress, establish by regulation standardized forms and procedures by which, at the time applications covering certain specified categories of nondramatic literary works are submitted for registration under section 408 of this title, the copyright owner may voluntarily grant to the Library of Congress a license to reproduce the copyrighted work by means of Braille or similar tactile symbols, or by fixation of a reading of the work in a phonorecord, or both, and to distribute the resulting copies or phonorecords solely for the use of the blind and physically handicapped and under limited conditions to be specified in the standardized forms.

710 Regulation:

201.15. Voluntary license to permit reproduction of nondramatic literary works solely for use of the blind and physically handicapped.

(a) General. (1) The "blind and physically handicapped" are persons elligible for special loan services of the Library of Congress, as designated by section 135a of title 2 of the United States Code as amended by Pub. L. 89-552 and regulations of the Library of Congress issued under that section.

(2) This section, and any license granted or exercised under this section, applies only to nondramatic literary works that have previously been published with the consent of the copyright owner.

(b) Form. The Copyright Office provides the following form as part of the applications for registration of claims to copyright in nondramatic literary works (Form TX):

Reproduction for Use of Blind or Physically Handicapped Persons

Signature of this form at space 10, and a check in one of the boxes here in space 8, constitutes a nonexclusive grant of permission to the Congress to reproduce and distribute solely for the blind and physically handicapped and under the conditions and limitations prescribed by the regulations of the Copyright Office: (1) copies of the work identified in space 1 of this application in Braille (or similar tactile symbols); or (2) phonorecords embodying a fixation of a reading of that work; or (3) both.

a ☐ Copies and phonorecords; b ☐ Copies only; c ☐ Phonorecords only.

(c) Terms and conditions. A copyright owner who consents to the use of a copyrighted work by the Library of Congress for the use of the blind and physically handicapped may accomplish this purpose by checking the appropriate box on the application form, by signing the application form as a whole, and by submitting the application for copyright registration to the Copyright Office. The copyright owner thereby grants a nonexclusive license to the Library of Congress with respect to the work identified in the application, under the terms and conditions set forth in this section.

(1) The work may be reproduced only by or on behalf of the Library of

Congress.

(2) The work may not be reproduced in any other form than Braille (or similar tactile symbols), or by a fixation of a reading of the work in phonorecords specifically designed for use of the blind and physically handicapped, or both, as designated by the copyright owner on the application form.

(3) Such copies and phonorecords of the work may be distributed by the Library of Congress solely for the use of the blind and physically handicapped under conditions and guidelines provided by the National Library Service for the Blind and Physically Handicapped of the Library of Congress.

(4) In the case of any conflict with any other right or license given by the copyright owner to the Library of Congress pertaining to the work, the terms and conditions most favorable to the Library of Congress for the benefit of the blind and physically handicapped shall govern.

(5) Copies and phonorecords reproduced and distributed under this license will contain identification of the author and publisher of the work, and copyright notice, as they appear on the copies or phonorecords deposited with the application.

(6) This license is nonexclusive, and the copyright is in no way precluded from granting other nonexclusive licenses with respect to reproduction for the use of the blind and physically handicapped, or exclusive licenses for the same purpose on condition they are subject to the nonexclusive license granted to the Library of Congress, or other exclusive or nonexclusive licenses or transfers with respect to reproduction or distribution for other purposes.

(7) All responsibility for the clearing and exercise of the rights granted is that of the Library of Congress.

(d) Duration of license. (1) The license is effective upon the effective date of registration for the work and, subject to the conditions and procedures stated in paragraph (d)(2) of this section, continues for the full term of copyright in the work provided in section 302 of title 17 of the United States Code as amended by Pub. L. 94-553.

(2) Termination of the license may be accomplished by the copyright owner at any time by submitting a written statement of intent to terminate, signed by the copyright owner or by the duly authorized agent of the copyright owner, to the National Library Service for the Blind and Physically Handicapped of the Library of Congress. Termination will become effective 90 days after receipt of the written statement, or at a later time set forth in the statement. Upon the effective date of termination the Library of Congress will be prohibited from reproducing additional copies or phonorecords of the work, or both, without the consent of the copyright owner, but copies or phonorecords, or both, reproduced under authority of the license before the effective date of termination may continue to be utilized and distributed under the terms of the license after its termination.

APPENDIX "A"

AUSTRALIA

"Division 5B—Copying of works in institutions assisting handicapped readers

Multiple copying under statutory licence by institutions assisting handicapped readers

"53D. (1) The copyright in a literary or dramatic work that has been published is not infringed by the making, by or on behalf of the body administering an institution assisting handicapped readers, of a record embodying a sound recording of the work or of a part of the work, for use by a handicapped reader for the purpose of research or study that he is undertaking or proposes to undertake, or for the purpose of otherwise instructing himself on any matter.

"(2) The copyright in a literary or dramatic work that has been published is not infringed by the making, by or on behalf of the body administering an institution assisting handicapped readers, of a Braille version, a large-print version or a photographic version, of the work or of a part of the work, for use taking or proposes to undertake, or for the purpose of otherwise instructing himself on any matter.

"(3) Where a sound recording of a work has been published, sub-section (1) does not apply to the making of any record embodying a sound recording of the work (including a record that is a copy of that first-mentioned sound recording) for or on behalf of the body administering an institution assisting handicapped readers unless the person who makes that record, or causes that record to be made, is satisfied, after reasonable investigation, that no new record that embodies only a sound recording of the work can be obtained within a reasonable time at an ordinary commercial price.

"(4) Where a Braille version of a work has been separately published, sub-section (2) does not apply to the making of a Braille version of the work, or of a part of the work, unless the person who makes that version, or causes that version to be made, for or on behalf of the body administering an institution assisting handicapped readers is satisfied, after reasonable investigation, that no new copy of a Braille version of the work, being a version that has been separately published, can be obtained within a reasonable time at an ordinary commercial price.

"(5) Where a large-print version of a work has been separately published, sub-section (2) does not apply to the making of a large-print version of the work, or of a part of the work, unless the person who makes the version, or causes the version to be made, for or on behalf of the body administering an institution assisting handicapped readers is satisfied, after reasonable investigation, that no new copy of a large-print version of the work, being a version that has been separately published, can be obtained within a reasonable time at an ordinary commercial price.

"(6) Where a photographic version of a work has been separately published, sub-section (2) does not apply to the making of a photographic version of the work, or of a part of the work, unless the person who makes the version, or causes the version to be made, for or on behalf of the body administering an institution assisting handicapped readers is satisfied, after reasonable investigation, that no new copy of a photographic version of the work, being a version that has been separately published, can be obtained within a reasonable time at an ordinary commercial price.

"(7) Sub-sections (1) and (2) do not apply to the reproduction of the whole or a part of an article contained in a periodical publication by way of the making, by or on behalf of the body administering an institution assisting handicapped readers, of a handicapped reader's copy of the article or of that part of the article unless there is made, by or on behalf of that body, as soon as practicable after the making of that copy, a record of the copying setting out—

(a) if the International Standard Serial Number in respect of the periodical publication is recorded in the periodical publication—that number;

(b) if the International Standard Serial Number in respect of the publication is not so recorded—the name of the periodical publication:

(c) the title or description of the article;

(d) the name of the author of the article (if that name is known);

(e) the volume, or volume and number, as the case requires, of the periodical publication containing the article;

(f) the page numbers of the pages in that volume, or in that number of that volume, that have been copied, or, in a case where a page so copied does not bear a page number, such description of the page as will enable it to be identified;

(g) the date on which the copy has been made;

(h) the form in which the copy has been made; and

(j) particulars of such other matters as are prescribed.

"(8) Sub-sections (1) and (2) do not apply to the reproduction of the whole or a part of a work (not being an article contained in a periodical publication) by way of the making, by or on behalf of the body administering an institution assisting handicapped readers, of a handicapped reader's copy of the work or of that part of the work unless there is made, by or on behalf of that body, as soon as practicable after the making of that copy, a record of the copying setting out—

(a) if the International Standard Book Number in respect of the work is recorded in the edition of the work copied—that number;

(b) if the International Standard Book Number in respect of the work is not so recorded—

(i) the title or description of the work;

(ii) the name of the publisher of the edition of the work; and

(iii) the name of the author of the work (if that name is known);

(c) the page numbers of the pages in the edition of the work that have been reproduced, or, in a case where a page so reproduced does not bear a page number, such description of the page as will enable it to be identified;

(d) the date on which the copy has been made;

(e) the form in which the copy has been made; and

(f) particulars of such other matters as are prescribed.

"(9) For the purposes of sub-sections (7) and (8), a record of the copying of a work or a part of a work—

(a) may be kept in writing or in any other manner prescribed by the regulations; and

(b) if it is kept in writing, shall be in accordance with the prescribed form.

"(10) Where a handicapped reader's copy of the whole or a part of a work is made by or on behalf of the body administering an institution assisting handicapped readers and, by virtue of this section, the making of that copy does not infringe copyright in the work, that body shall, if the owner of the copyright in the work makes a request, in writing, at any time during the prescribed period after the making of the copy, for payment for the making of the copy, pay to the owner such an amount by way of equitable remuneration for the making of that copy as is agreed upon between the owner and the body, or, in default of agreement, such amount as is determined by the Copyright Tribunal on the application of either the owner or the body.

"(11) Where the Copyright Tribunal has determined the amount of equitable remuneration payable to the owner of copyright in a work by the body administering an institution assisting handicapped readers in relation to a handicapped reader's copy of the whole or a part of that work that has been made by or on behalf of that body in reliance on this section, the owner may recover that amount from the body in a court of competent jurisdiction as a debt due to him.

"(12) Notwithstanding any other provision of this Act, copyright shall not vest in the maker of the handicapped reader's copy by reason of his making that copy.

"(13) Nothing in this section affects the right of the owner of copyright in a work to grant a licence authorizing the body administering an institution assisting handicapped readers to make, or cause to be made, sound recordings of, or Braille, large-print or photographic versions of, the whole or a part of the work without infringement of that copyright.

"(14) For the purposes of this section, a record, or a Braille version, a large-print version or a photographic version, of a work shall be taken to be a new record, or a new Braille version, a new large-print version or a new photographic version, of the work, as the case may be, if it is not a second-hand record, or a second-hand Braille version, a second-hand large-print version or a second-hand photographic version, of the work, as the case may be.

"(15) In this section, a reference to a photographic version of a work or a part of a work shall be read as a reference to a copy or copies of the work or a part of a work produced as a film-strip or series of separate transparencies designed to meet the needs of handicapped readers.".

15. Section 104 of the Principal Act is repealed and the following section substituted:

Acts done for purposes of judicial proceeding

"104. A copyright subsisting by virtue of this Part is not infringed by anything done—

(a) for the purpose of a judicial proceeding or a report of a judicial proceeding;

(b) for the purpose of seeking professional advice from a legal practitioner or patent attorney; or

(c) for the purpose of, or in the course of, the giving of professional advice by a legal practitioner or patent attorney.".

APPENDIX "B"

Berne Convention For the Protection of Literary and Artistic Works Paris Act, 1971

Article 9

(1) Authors of literary and artistic works protected by this Convention shall have the exclusive right of authorizing the reproduction of these works, in any manner or form.

(2) It shall be a matter for legislation in the countries of the Union to permit the reproduction of such works in certain special cases, provided that such reproduction does not conflict with a normal exploitation of the work and does not unreasonably prejudice the legitimate interests of the author.

(3) Any sound or visual recording shall be considered as a reproduction for the purposes of this Convention.

Article 10

(1) It shall be permissible to make quotations from a work which has already been lawfully made available to the public, provided that their making is compatible with fair practice, and their extent does not exceed that justified by the purpose, including quotations from newspaper articles and periodicals in the form of press summaries.

(2) It shall be a matter for legislation in the countries of the Union, and for special agreements existing or to be concluded between them, to permit the utilization, to the extent justified by the purpose, of literary or artistic works by way of illustration in publications, broadcasts or sound or visual recordings for teaching, provided such utilization is compatible with fair practice.

(3) Where use is made of works in accordance with the preceding paragraphs of this Article, mention shall be made of the source, and of the name of the author if it appears thereon.

Article 11

(1) Authors of dramatic, dramatico-musical and musical works shall enjoy the exclusive right of authorizing:

(i) the public performance of their works, including such public performance by any means or process;

(ii) any communication to the public of the performance of their works.

(2) Authors of dramatic or dramatico-musical works shall enjoy, during the full term of their rights in the original works, the same rights with respect to translations thereof.

Article 11bis

(1) Authors of literary and artistic works shall enjoy the exclusive right of authorizing:

(i) the broadcasting of their works or the communication thereof to the public by any other means of wireless diffusion of signs, sounds or images;

(ii) any communication to the public by wire or by rebroadcasting of the broadcast of the work, when this communication is made by an organization other than the original one;

(iii) the public communication by loudspeaker or any other analogous instrument transmitting, by signs, sounds or images, the broadcast of the work.

(2) It shall be a matter for legislation in the countries of the Union to determine the conditions under which the rights mentioned in the preceding paragraph may be exercised, but these conditions shall apply only in the countries where they have been prescribed. They shall not in any circumstances be prejudicial to the moral rights of the author, nor to his right to obtain equitable remuneration which, in the absence of agreement, shall be fixed by competent authority.

(3) In the absence of any contrary stipulation, permission granted in accordance with paragraph (1) of this Article shall not imply permission to record, by means of instruments recording sounds or images, the work broadcast. It shall, however, be a matter for legislation in the countries of the Union to determine the regulations for ephemeral recordings made by a broadcasting organization by means of its own facilities and used for its own broadcasts. The preservation of these recordings in official archives may, on the ground of their exceptional documentary character, be authorized by such legislation.

Article 11ter

(1) Authors of literary works shall enjoy the exclusive right of authorizing:

(i) the public recitation of their works, including such public recitation by any means or process;

(ii) any communication to the public of the recitation of their works.

(2) Authors of literary works shall enjoy, during the full term of their rights in the original works, the same rights with respect to translations thereof.

Article 13

(1) Each country of the Union may impose for itself reservations and conditions on the exclusive right granted to the author of a musical work and to the author of any words,

the recording of which together with the musical work has already been authorized by the latter, to authorize the sound recording of that musical work, together with such words, if any; but all such reservations and conditions shall apply only in the countries which have imposed them and shall not, in any circumstances, be prejudicial to the rights of these authors to obtain equitable remuneration which, in the absence of agreement, shall be fixed by competent authority.

(2) Recordings of musical works made in a country of the Union in accordance with Article 13(3) of the Conventions signed at Rome on June 2, 1928, and at Brussels on June 26, 1948, may be reproduced in that country without the permission of the author of the musical work until a date two years after that country becomes bound by this Act.

(3) Recordings made in accordance with paragraphs (1) and (2) of this Article and imported without permission from the parties concerned into a country where they are treated as infringing recordings shall be liable to seizure.

Article 21

(1) Special provisions regarding developing countries are included in the Appendix.

(2) Subject to the provisions of Article 28(1)*(b)*, the Appendix forms an integral part of this Act.

APPENDIX

Article I

(1) Any country regarded as a developing country in conformity with the established practice of the General Assembly of the United Nations which ratifies or accedes to this Act, of which this Appendix forms an integral part, and which, having regard to its economic situation and its social or cultural needs, does not consider itself immediately in a position to make provision for the protection of all the rights as pro-

vided for in this Act, may, by a notification deposited with the Director General at the time of depositing its instrument of ratification or accession or, subject to Article V(1)*(c)*, at any time thereafter, declare that it will avail itself of the faculty provided for in Article II, or of the faculty provided for in Article III, or of both of those faculties. It may, instead of availing itself of the faculty provided for in Article II, make a declaration according to Article V(1)*(a)*.

(2) *(a)* Any declaration under paragraph (1) notified before the expiration of the period of ten years from the entry into force of Articles 1 to 21 and this Appendix according to Article 28(2) shall be effective until the expiration of the said period. Any such declaration may be renewed in whole or in part for periods of ten years each by a notification deposited with the Director General not more than fifteen months and not less than three months before the expiration of the ten-year period then running.

(b) Any declaration under paragraph (1) notified after the expiration of the period of ten years from the entry into force of Articles 1 to 21 and this Appendix according to Article 28(2) shall be effective until the expiration of the ten-year period then running. Any such declaration may be renewed as provided for in the second sentence of subparagraph *(a)*.

(3) Any country of the Union which has ceased to be regarded as a developing country as referred to in paragraph (1) shall no longer be entitled to renew its declaration as provided in paragraph (2), and, whether or not it formally withdraws its declaration, such country shall be precluded from availing itself of the faculties referred to in paragraph (1) from the expiration of the ten-year period then running or from the expiration of a period of three years after it has ceased to be regarded as a developing country, whichever period expires later.

(4) Where, at the time when the declaration made under paragraph (1) or (2) ceases to be effective, there are copies in stock which were made under a license granted by virtue of this Appendix, such copies may continue to be distributed until their stock is exhausted.

(5) Any country which is bound by the provisions of this Act and which has deposited a declaration or a notification in accordance with Article 31(1) with respect to the application of this Act to a particular territory, the situation of which can be regarded as analogous to that of the countries referred to in paragraph (1), may, in respect of such territory, make the declaration referred to in paragraph (1) and the notification of renewal referred to in paragraph (2). As long as such declaration or notification remains in effect, the provisions of this Appendix shall be applicable to the territory in respect of which it was made.

(6) *(a)* The fact that a country avails itself of any of the faculties referred to in paragraph (1) does not permit another country to give less protection to works of which the country of origin is the former country than it is obliged to grant under Articles 1 to 20.

(b) The right to apply reciprocal treatment provided for in Article 30(2)*(b)*, second sentence, shall not, until the date on which the period applicable under Article I(3) expires, be exercised in respect of works the country of origin of which is a country which has made a declaration according to Article V(1)*(a)*.

Article II

(1) Any country which has declared that it will avail itself of the faculty provided for in this Article shall be entitled, so far as works published in printed or analogous forms of reproduction are concerned, to substitute for the

exclusive right of translation provided for in Article 8 a system of non-exclusive and non-transferable licenses, granted by the competent authority under the following conditions and subject to Article IV.

(2) *(a)* Subject to paragraph (3), if, after the expiration of a period of three years, or of any longer period determined by the national legislation of the said country, commencing on the date of the first publication of the work, a translation of such work has not been published in a language in general use in that country by the owner of the right of translation, or with his authorization, any national of such country may obtain a license to make a translation of the work in the said language and publish the translation in printed or analogous forms of reproduction.

(b) A license under the conditions provided for in this Article may also be granted if all the editions of the translation published in the language concerned are out of print.

(3)*(a)* In the case of translations into a language which is not in general use in one or more developed countries which are members of the Union, a period of one year shall be substituted for the period of three years referred to in paragraph (2)*(a)*.

(b) Any country referred to in paragraph (1) may, with the unanimous agreement of the developed countries which are members of the Union and in which the same language is in general use, substitute, in the case of translations into that language, for the period of three years referred to in paragraph (2)*(a)* a shorter period as determined by such agreement but not less than one year. However, the provisions of the foregoing sentence shall not apply where the language in question is English, French or Spanish. The Director General shall be notified of any such agreement by the Governments which have concluded it.

(4) *(a)* No license obtainable after three years shall be granted under this Article until a further period of six months has elapsed, and no license obtainable after one year shall be granted under this Article until a further period of nine months has elapsed

(i) from the date on which the applicant complies with the requirements mentioned in Article IV(1), or

(ii) where the identity or the address of the owner of the right of translation is unknown, from the date on which the applicant sends, as provided for in Article IV(2), copies of his application submitted to the authority competent to grant the license.

(b) If, during the said period of six or nine months, a translation in the language in respect of which the application was made is published by the owner of the right of translation or with his authorization, no license under this Article shall be granted.

(5) Any license under this Article shall be granted only for the purpose of teaching, scholarship or research.

(6) If a translation of a work is published by the owner of the right of translation or with his authorization at a price reasonably related to that normally charged in the country for comparable works, any license granted under this Article shall terminate if such translation is in the same language and with substantially the same content as the translation published under the license. Any copies already made before the license terminates may continue to be distributed until their stock is exhausted.

(7) For works which are composed mainly of illustrations, a license to make and publish a translation of the text and to reproduce and publish the illustrations may be granted only if the conditions of Article III are also fulfilled.

(8) No license shall be granted under this Article when the author has withdrawn from circulation all copies of his work.

(9) *(a)* A license to make a translation of a work which has been published in printed or analogous forms of reproduction may also be granted to any broadcasting organization having its headquarters in a country referred to in paragraph (1), upon an application made to the competent authority of that country by the said organization, provided that all of the following conditions are met:

(i) the translation is made from a copy made and acquired in accordance with the laws of the said country;

(ii) the translation is only for use in broadcasts intended exclusively for teaching or for the dissemination of the results of specialized technical or scientific research to experts in a particular profession;

(iii) the translation is used exclusively for the purposes referred to in condition (ii) through broadcasts made lawfully and intended for recipients on the territory of the said country, including broadcasts made through the medium of sound or visual recordings lawfully and exclusively made for the purpose of such broadcasts;

(iv) all uses made of the translation are without any commercial purpose.

(b) Sound or visual recordings of a translation which was made by a broadcasting organization under a license granted by virtue of this paragraph may, for the purposes and subject to the conditions referred to in subparagraph *(a)* and with the agreement of that organization, also be used by any other broadcasting organization having its headquarters in the country whose competent authority granted the license in question.

(c) Provided that all of the criteria and conditions set out in subparagraph *(a)* are met, a license may also be granted to a broadcasting organization to translate any text incorporated in an audio-visual fixation where such fixation was itself prepared and published for the sole purpose of being used in connection with systematic instructional activities.

(d) Subject to subparagraphs *(a)* to *(c)*, the provisions of the preceding paragraphs shall apply to the grant and exercise of any license granted under this paragraph.

Article III

(1) Any country which has declared that it will avail itself of the faculty provided for in this Article shall be entitled to substitute for the exclusive right of reproduction provided for in Article 9 a system of non-exclusive and non-transferable licenses, granted by the competent authority under the following conditions and subject to Article IV.

(2) *(a)* If, in relation to a work to which this Article applies by virtue of paragraph (7), after the expiration of

(i) the relevant period specified in paragraph (3), commencing on the date of first publication of a particular edition of the work, or

(ii) any longer period determined by national legislation of the country referred to in paragraph (1), commencing on the same date,

copies of such edition have not been distributed in that country to the general public or in connection with systematic instructional activities, by the owner of the right of reproduction or with his authorization, at a price reasonably related to that normally charged in the country for comparable works, any national of such country may obtain a license to reproduce and publish such edition at that or a lower price for use in connection with systematic instructional activities.

(b) A license to reproduce and publish an edition which has been distributed as described in subparagraph *(a)* may also be granted under the conditions provided for in this Article if, after the expiration of the applicable period, no authorized copies of that edition have been on sale for a period of six months in the country concerned to the general public or in connection with systematic instructional activities at a price reasonably related to that normally charged in the country for comparable works.

(3) The period referred to in paragraph (2)*(a)*(i) shall be five years, except that

(i) for works of the natural and physical sciences, including mathematics, and of technology, the period shall be three years;

(ii) for works of fiction, poetry, drama and music, and for art books, the period shall be seven years.

(4) *(a)* No license obtainable after three years shall be granted under this Article until a period of six months has elapsed

(i) from the date on which the applicant complies with the requirements mentioned in Article IV(1), or

(ii) where the identity or the address of the owner of the right of reproduction is unknown, from the date on which the applicant sends, as provided for in Article IV(2), copies of his application submitted to the authority competent to grant the license.

(b) Where licenses are obtainable after other periods and Article IV(2) is applicable, no license shall be granted until a period of three months has elapsed from the date of the dispatch of the copies of the application.

(c) If, during the period of six or three months referred to in subparagraphs *(a)* and *(b)*, a distribution as described in paragraph (2)*(a)* has taken place, no license shall be granted under this Article.

(d) No license shall be granted if the author has withdrawn from circulation all copies of the edition for the reproduction and publication of which the license has been applied for.

(5) A license to reproduce and publish a translation of a work shall not be granted under this Article in the following cases:

(i) where the translation was not published by the owner of the right of translation or with his authorization, or

(ii) where the translation is not in a language in general use in the country in which the license is applied for.

(6) If copies of an edition of a work are distributed in the country referred to in paragraph (1) to the general public or in connection with systematic instructional activities, by the owner of the right of reproduction or with his authorization, at a price reasonably related to that normally charged in the country for comparable works, any license granted under this Article shall terminate if such edition is in the same language and with substantially the same content as the edition which was published under the said license. Any copies already made before the license terminates may continue to be distributed until their stock is exhausted.

(7) *(a)* Subject to subparagraph *(b)*, the works to which this Article applies shall be limited to works published in printed or analogous forms of reproduction.

(b) This Article shall also apply to the reproduction in audio-visual form of lawfully made audio-visual fixations including any protected works incorporated therein and to the translation of any incorporated text into a language in general use in the country in which the license is applied for, always provided that the audio-visual fixations in question were prepared and published for the sole purpose of being used in connection with systematic instructional activities.

Article IV

(1) A license under Article II or Article III may be granted only if the applicant, in accordance with the procedure of the country concerned, establishes either that he has requested, and has been denied, authorization by the owner of the right to make and publish the translation or to reproduce and publish the edition, as the case may be, or that, after due diligence on his part, he was unable to find the owner of the right. At the same time as making the request, the applicant shall inform any national or international information center referred to in paragraph (2).

(2) If the owner of the right cannot be found, the applicant for a license shall send, by registered airmail, copies of his application, submitted to the authority competent to grant the license, to the publisher whose name appears on the work and to any national or international information center which may have been designated, in a notification to that effect deposited with the Director General, by the Government of the country in which the publisher is believed to have his principal place of business.

(3) The name of the author shall be indicated on all copies of the translation or reproduction published under a license granted under Article II or Article III. The title of the work shall appear on all such copies. In the case of a translation, the original title of the work shall appear in any case on all the said copies.

(4) *(a)* No license granted under Article II or Article III shall extend to the export of copies, and any such license shall be valid only for publication of the translation or of the reproduction, as the case may be, in the territory of the country in which it has been applied for.

(b) For the purposes of subparagraph *(a)*, the notion of export shall include the sending of copies from any territory to the country which, in respect of that territory, has made a declaration under Article I(5).

(c) Where a governmental or other public entity of a country which has granted a license to make a translation under Article II into a language other than English, French or Spanish sends copies of a translation published under such license to another country, such sending of copies shall not, for the purposes of subparagraph *(a)*, be considered to constitute export if all of the following conditions are met:

(i) the recipients are individuals who are nationals of the country whose competent authority has granted the license, or organizations grouping such individuals;

(ii) the copies are to be used only for the purpose of teaching, scholarship or research;

(iii) the sending of the copies and their subsequent distribution to recipients is without any commercial purpose; and

(iv) the country to which the copies have been sent has agreed with the country whose competent authority has granted the license to allow the receipt, or distribution, or both, and the Director General has been notified of the agreement by the Government of the country in which the license has been granted.

(5) All copies published under a license granted by virtue of Article II or Article III shall bear a notice in the appropriate language stating that the copies are available for distribution only in the country or territory to which the said license applies.

(6) *(a)* Due provision shall be made at the national level to ensure

(i) that the license provides, in favour of the owner of the right of translation or of reproduction, as the case may be, for just compensation that is consistent with standards of royalties normally operating on licenses freely negotiated between persons in the two countries concerned, and

(ii) payment and transmittal of the compensation: should national currency regulations intervene, the competent authority shall make all efforts, by the use of international machinery, to ensure transmittal in internationally convertible currency or its equivalent.

(b) Due provision shall be made by national legislation to ensure a correct translation of the work, or an accurate reproduction of the particular edition, as the case may be.

Article V

(1) *(a)* Any country entitled to make a declaration that it will avail itself of the faculty provided for in Article II may, instead, at the time of ratifying or acceding to this Act:

(i) if it is a country to which Article 30(2)*(a)* applies, make a declaration under that provision as far as the right of translation is concerned;

(ii) if it is a country to which Article 30(2)*(a)* does not apply, and even if it is not a country outside the Union, make a declaration as provided for in Article 30(2)*(b)*, first sentence.

(b) In the case of a country which ceases to be regarded as a developing country as referred to in Article I(1), a declaration made according to this paragraph shall be effective until the date on which the period applicable under Article I(3) expires.

(c) Any country which has made a declaration according to this paragraph may not subsequently avail itself of the faculty provided for in Article II even if it withdraws the said declaration.

(2) Subject to paragraph (3), any country which has availed itself of the faculty provided for in Article II may not subsequently make a declaration according to paragraph (1).

(3) Any country which has ceased to be regarded as a developing country as referred to in Article I(1) may, not later than two years prior to the expiration of the period applicable under Article I(3), make a declaration to the effect provided for in Article 30(2)*(b)*, first sentence, notwithstanding the fact that it is not a country outside the Union. Such declaration shall take effect at the date on which the period applicable under Article I(3) expires.

Article VI

(1) Any country of the Union may declare, as from the date of this Act, and at any time before becoming bound by Articles 1 to 21 and this Appendix:

(i) if it is a country which, were it bound by Articles 1 to 21 and this Appendix, would be entitled to avail itself of the faculties referred to in Article I(1), that it will apply the provisions of Article II or of Article III or of both to works whose country of origin is a country which, pursuant to (ii) below, admits the application of those Articles to such works, or which is bound by Articles 1 to 21 and this Appendix; such declaration may, instead of referring to Article II, refer to Article V;

(ii) that it admits the application of this Appendix to works of which it is the country of origin by countries which have made a declaration under (i) above or a notification under Article I.

(2) Any declaration made under paragraph (1) shall be in writing and shall be deposited with the Director General The declaration shall become effective from the date of its deposit.

APPENDIX "C"

Universal Copyright Convention
Paris Act, 1971

Article I

Each Contracting State undertakes to provide for the adequate and effective protection of the rights of authors and other copyright proprietors in literary, scientific and artistic works, including writings, musical, dramatic and cinematographic works, and paintings, engravings and sculpture.

*Article IV*bis

1. The rights referred to in Article I shall include the basic rights ensuring the author's economic interests, including the exclusive right to authorize reproduction by any means, public performance and broadcasting. The provisions of this Article shall extend to works protected under this Convention either in their original form or in any form recognizably derived from the original.
2. However, any Contracting State may, by its domestic legislation, make exceptions that do not conflict with the spirit and provisions of this Convention, to the rights mentioned in paragraph 1 of this Article. Any State whose legislation so provides, shall nevertheless accord a reasonable degree of effective protection to each of the rights to which exception has been made.

Article V

1. The rights referred to in Article I shall include the exclusive right of the author to make, publish and authorize the making and publication of translations of works protected under this Convention.
2. However, any Contracting State may, by its domestic legislation, restrict the right of translation of writings, but only subject to the following provisions:
   (a) If, after the expiration of a period of seven years from the date of the first publication of a writing, a translation of such writing has not been published in a language in general use in the Contracting State, by the owner of the right of translation or with his authorization, any national of such Contracting State may obtain a non-exclusive licence from the competent authority thereof to translate the work into that language and publish the work so translated.
   (b) Such national shall in accordance with the procedure of the State concerned, establish either that he has requested, and been denied, authorization by the proprietor of the right to make and publish the translation, or that, after due diligence on his part, he was unable to find the owner of the right. A licence may also be granted on the same conditions if all previous editions of a translation in a language in general use in the Contracting State are out of print.
   (c) If the owner of the right of translation cannot be found, then the applicant for a licence shall send copies of his application to the publisher whose name appears on the work and, if the nationality of the owner of the right of translation is known, to the diplomatic or consular representative of the State of which such owner is a national, or to the organization which may have been designated by the government of that State. The licence shall not be granted before the expiration of a period of two months from the date of the dispatch of the copies of the application.
   (d) Due provision shall be made by domestic legislation to ensure to the owner of the right of translation a compensation which is just and conforms to international standards, to ensure payment and transmittal of such compensation, and to ensure a correct translation of the work.
   (e) The original title and the name of the author of the work shall be printed on all copies of the published translation. The licence shall be valid only for publication of the translation in the territory of the Contracting State where it has been applied for. Copies so published may be imported and sold in another Contracting State if a language in general use in such other State is the same language as that into which the work has been so translated, and if the domestic law in such other State makes provision for such licences and does not prohibit such importation and sale. Where the foregoing conditions do not exist, the importation and sale of such copies in a Contracting State shall be governed by its domestic law and its agreements. The licence shall not be transferred by the licensee.
   (f) The licence shall not be granted when the author has withdrawn from circulation all copies of the work.

Article Vbis

1. Any Contracting State regarded as a developing country in conformity with the established practice of the General Assembly of the United Nations may, by a notification deposited with the Director-General of the United Nations Educational, Scientific and Cultural Organization (hereinafter called 'the Director-General') at the time of its ratification, acceptance or accession or thereafter, avail itself of any or all of the exceptions provided for in Articles V*ter* and V*quater*.
2. Any such notification shall be effective for ten years from the date of coming into force of this Convention, or for such part of that ten-year period as remains at the date of deposit of the notification, and may be renewed in whole or in part for further periods of ten years each if, not more than fifteen or less than three months before the expiration of the relevant ten-year period, the Contracting State deposits a further notification with the Director-General. Initial notifications may also be made during these further periods of ten years in accordance with the provisions of this Article.
3. Notwithstanding the provisions of paragraph 2, a Contracting State that has ceased to be regarded as a developing country as referred to in paragraph 1 shall no longer be entitled to renew its notification made under the provisions of paragraph 1 or 2, and whether or not it formally withdraws the notification such State shall be precluded from availing itself of the exceptions provided for in Articles V*ter* and V*quater* at the end of the current ten-year period, or at the end of three years after it has ceased to be regarded as a developing country, whichever period expires later.
4. Any copies of a work already made under the exceptions provided for in Articles V*ter* and V*quater* may continue to be distributed after the expiration of the period for which notifications under this Article were effective until their stock is exhausted.
5. Any Contracting State that has deposited a notification in accordance with Article XIII with respect to the application of this Convention to a particular country or territory, the situation of which can be regarded as analogous to that of the States referred to in paragraph 1 of this Article, may also deposit notifications and renew them in accordance with the provisions of this Article with respect to any such country or territory. During the effective period of such notifications, the provisions of Articles V*ter* and V*quater* may be applied with respect to such country or territory. The sending of copies from the country or territory to the Contracting State shall be considered as export within the meaning of Articles V*ter* and V*quater*.

Article Vter

1. (a) Any Contracting State to which Article V*bis* (1) applies may substitute for the period of seven years provided for in Article V (2) a period of three years or any longer period prescribed by its legislation. However, in the case of a translation into a language not in general use in one or more developed countries that are party to this Convention or only the 1952 Convention, the period shall be one year instead of three.

(b) A Contracting State to which Article V*bis* (1) applies may, with the unanimous agreement of the developed countries party to this Convention or only the 1952 Convention and in which the same language is in general use, substitute, in the case of translation into that language, for the period of three years provided for in sub-paragraph (a) another period as determined by such agreement but not shorter than one year. However, this sub-paragraph shall not apply where the language in question is English, French or Spanish. Notification of any such agreement shall be made to the Director-General.

(c) The licence may only be granted if the applicant, in accordance with the procedure of the State concerned, establishes either that he has requested, and been denied, authorization by the owner of the right of translation, or that, after due diligence on his part, he was unable to find the owner of the right. At the same time as he makes his request he shall inform either the International Copyright Information Centre established by the United Nations Educational, Scientific and Cultural Organization or any national or regional information centre which may have been designated in a notification to that effect deposited with the Director-General by the government of the State in which the publisher is believed to have his principal place of business.

Article Vquater

1. Any Contracting State to which Article V*bis* (1) applies may adopt the following provisions:

(a) If, after the expiration of (i) the relevant period specified in sub-paragraph (c) commencing from the date of first publication of a particular edition of a literary, scientific or artistic work referred to in paragraph 3, or (ii) any longer period determined by national legislation of the State, copies of such edition have not been distributed in that State to the general public or in connexion with systematic instructional activities at a price reasonably related to that normally charged in the State for comparable works, by the owner of the right of reproduction or with his authorization, any national of such State may obtain a non-exclusive licence from the competent authority to publish such edition at that or a lower price for use in connexion with systematic instructional activities. The licence may only be granted if such national, in accordance with the procedure of the State concerned, establishes either that he has requested, and been denied, authorization by the proprietor of the right to publish such work, or that, after due diligence on his part, he was unable to find the owner of the right. At the same time as he makes his request he shall inform either the international copyright information centre established by the United Nations Educational, Scientific and Cultural Organization or any national or regional information centre referred to in sub-paragraph (d).

(b) A licence may also be granted on the same conditions if, for a period of six months, no authorized copies of the edition in question have been on sale in the State concerned to the general public or in connexion with systematic instructional activities at a price reasonably related to that normally charged in the State for comparable works.

(c) The period referred to in sub-paragraph (a) shall be five years except that:

(i) for works of the natural and physical sciences, including mathematics, and of technology, the period shall be three years;

(ii) for works of fiction, poetry, drama and music, and for art books, the period shall be seven years.

(d) If the owner of the right of reproduction cannot be found, the applicant for a licence shall send, by registered air mail, copies of his application to the publisher whose name appears on the work and to any national or regional information centre identified as such in a notification deposited with the Director-General by the State in which the publisher is believed to have his principal place of business. In the absence of any such notification, he shall also send a copy to the international copyright information centre established by the United Nations Educational, Scientific and Cultural Organization. The licence shall not be granted before the expiration of a period of three months from the date of dispatch of the copies of the application.

(e) Licences obtainable after three years shall not be granted under this Article:

(i) until a period of six months has elapsed from the date of the request for permission referred to in sub-paragraph (a) or, if the identity or address of the owner of the right of reproduction is unknown, from the date of the dispatch of the copies of the application for a licence referred to in sub-paragraph (d);

(ii) if any such distribution of copies of the edition as is mentioned in sub-paragraph (a) has taken place during that period.

(f) The name of the author and the title of the particular edition of the work shall be printed on all copies of the published reproduction. The licence shall not extend to the export of copies and shall be valid only for publication in the territory of the Contracting State where it has been applied for. The licence shall not be transferable by the licensee.

(g) Due provision shall be made by domestic legislation to ensure an accurate reproduction of the particular edition in question.

(h) A licence to reproduce and publish a translation of a work shall not be granted under this Article in the following cases:

(i) where the translation was not published by the owner of the right of translation or with his authorization;

(ii) where the translation is not in a language in general use in the State with power to grant the licence.

2. The exceptions provided for in paragraph 1 are subject to the following additional provisions:

(a) Any copy published in accordance with a licence granted under this Article shall bear a notice in the appropriate language stating that the copy is available for distribution only in the Contracting State to which the said licence applies. If the edition bears the notice specified in Article III (1), the copies shall bear the same notice.

(b) Due provision shall be made at the national level to ensure:

(i) that the licence provides for just compensation that is consistent with standards of royalties normally operating in the case of licences freely negotiated between persons in the two countries concerned; and

(ii) payment and transmittal of the compensation; however, should national currency regulations intervene, the competent authority shall make all efforts, by the use of international machinery, to ensure transmittal in internationally convertible currency or its equivalent.

(c) Whenever copies of an edition of a work are distributed in the Contracting State to the general public or in connexion with systematic instructional activities, by the owner of the right of reproduction or with his authorization, at a price reasonably related to that normally charged in the State for comparable works, any licence granted under this Article shall terminate if such edition is in the same language and is substantially the same in content as the edition published under the licence. Any copies already made before the licence is terminated may continue to be distributed until their stock is exhausted.

(d) No licence shall be granted when the author has withdrawn from circulation all copies of the edition in question.

3. (a) Subject to sub-paragraph (b), the literary, scientific or artistic works to which this Article applies shall be limited to works published in printed or analogous forms of reproduction.

(b) The provisions of this Article shall also apply to reproduction in audio-visual form of lawfully made audio-visual fixations including any protected works incorporated therein and to the translation of any incorporated text into a language in general use in the State with power to grant the licence; always provided that the audio-visual fixations in question were prepared and published for the sole purpose of being used in connexion with systematic instructional activities.

Bei Fragen zur Produktsicherheit wenden Sie sich bitte an:
If you have any questions regarding product safety,
please contact:

Walter de Gruyter GmbH
Genthiner Straße 13
10785 Berlin
productsafety@degruyterbrill.com